Sustainability and Environment

ISSUES

Volume 146

Editors

Cobi Smith and Lisa Firth

Independence
Educational Publishers
Cambridge

First published by Independence
The Studio, High Green
Great Shelford
Cambridge CB22 5EG
England

© Independence 2008

British Library Cataloguing in Publication Data
Sustainability and Environment – (Issues Series)
I. Smith, Cobi II. Series
363.7

ISBN 978 1 86168 419 6

Printed in Great Britain
MWL Print Group Ltd

Cover
The illustration on the front cover is by
Simon Kneebone.

CONTENTS

Chapter One: Defining Sustainability

Environmental sustainability 1

Fast facts: environmental sustainability 2

What is sustainable development? 3

The UK's ecological debt 4

Sustainable consumption and production 7

Securing the future 8

What are natural resources? 9

Ecological Footprint 10

Sustainable construction 11

Chapter Two: Sustainability Challenges

Population, poverty and the environment 12

The water crisis 13

2.6 billion wait in line for toilets 14

Plumbing beats penicillin 15

Environmental migration 16

Urban growth and sustainable use of space 17

Sustaining life on earth 18

Your natural heritage: why it matters 21

Contaminated land 22

Britain: the 'dustbin of Europe' 23

Intrusion 24

Agricultural land use 25

What is organic? 25

Return of GM 26

GM food: the solutions 27

Fisheries 28

Better buys: what fish can I eat? 29

Forests 30

Conservation 32

EU: top global importer of wildlife 34

Air pollution 35

Pollution putting groundwater supplies at risk, warns agency 36

Why monitor air pollution? 37

Can shopping save the planet? 38

Key Facts 40

Glossary 41

Index 42

Additional Resources 43

Acknowledgements 44

Useful information for readers

Dear Reader,

Issues: Sustainability and Environment

In many ways, 'sustainability' is the buzz word for a new millennium. As our stocks of finite resources run dangerously low, levels of production and consumption become ever higher. And while trends show that we are making the effort to live greener lives, the problem of pollution has not gone away, with the UK dumping more household waste into landfill than any other EU country. Will our environmental legacy survive? This book explores the issues involved.

The purpose of *Issues*

Sustainability and Environment is the one hundred and forty-sixth volume in the **Issues** series. The aim of this series is to offer up-to-date information about important issues in our world. Whether you are a regular reader or new to the series, we do hope you find this book a useful overview of the many and complex issues involved in the topic.

Titles in the **Issues** series are resource books designed to be of especial use to those undertaking project work or requiring an overview of facts, opinions and information on a particular subject, particularly as a prelude to undertaking their own research.

The information in this book is not from a single author, publication or organisation; the value of this unique series lies in the fact that it presents information from a wide variety of sources, including:
⇨ Government reports and statistics
⇨ Newspaper articles and features
⇨ Information from think-tanks and policy institutes
⇨ Magazine features and surveys
⇨ Website material
⇨ Literature from lobby groups and charitable organisations. *

Critical evaluation

Because the information reprinted here is from a number of different sources, readers should bear in mind the origin of the text and whether the source is likely to have a particular bias or agenda when presenting information (just as they would if undertaking their own research). It is hoped that, as you read about the many aspects of the issues explored in this book, you will critically evaluate the information presented. It is important that you decide whether you are being presented with facts or opinions. Does the writer give a biased or an unbiased report? If an opinion is being expressed, do you agree with the writer?

Sustainability and Environment offers a useful starting point for those who need convenient access to information about the many issues involved. However, it is only a starting point. Following each article is a URL to the relevant organisation's website, which you may wish to visit for further information.

Kind regards,

Lisa Firth
Editor, **Issues** series

** Please note that Independence Publishers has no political affiliations or opinions on the topics covered in the **Issues** series, and any views quoted in this book are not necessarily those of the publisher or its staff.*

Environmental sustainability

Millennium Development Goal 7. Information from the UN Millennium Campaign

Introduction

Reducing poverty and achieving sustained development must be done in conjunction with a healthy planet. The Millennium Goals recognise that environmental sustainability is part of global economic and social well-being. Unfortunately exploitation of natural resources such as forests, land, water, and fisheries – often by the powerful few – has caused alarming changes in our natural world in recent decades, often harming the most vulnerable people in the world who depend on natural resources for their livelihood.

The targets

Goal 7 of the Millennium Development Goals sets out by the year 2015 to:

⇨ Integrate the principles of sustainable development into country policies and programmes; reverse loss of environmental resources.

⇨ Reduce by half the proportion of people without sustainable access to safe drinking water.

⇨ Achieve significant improvement in lives of at least 100 million slum dwellers, by 2020.

Did you know?

In our world today around 2.5 billion people do not have access to improved sanitation and some 1.2 billion people do not have access to an improved source of water. (Source: *Why do the Millennium Development Goals matter?* Brochure)

About the Millennium Development Goals

When 189 Heads of State and government from the North and South, as representatives of their citizens, signed onto the Millennium Declaration at the 2000 UN Millennium Summit, there was a palpable sense of urgency. Urgency

to 'free our fellow men, women and children from the abject and dehumanising conditions of extreme poverty, to which more than a billion of them are currently subjected'.

> **Reducing poverty and achieving sustained development must be done in conjunction with a healthy planet**

Achieving the goals

Today, we not only have the financial resources to end extreme poverty once and for all, but we have the technological knowledge and know-how to realise the Goals. It is also clear, however, that if we carry on in a 'business as usual' mode, the Goals will not be achieved by 2015. The way forward is marked, it is only the political will to achieve the Goals that is in question.

What's different this time?

Given the proliferation of UN Conferences and commitments, it's important to understand why the Millennium Goals are unique in many powerful ways:

⇨ They represent a compact between all the world's major economic players. Poorer countries pledged to improve policies and governance and increase accountability to their own citizens; wealthy countries pledged to provide the resources. Since the commitment to achieve the goals comes from the highest political levels, for the first time, entire governments are committed to their achievement – including the trade and finance ministers who hold the world's purse strings. And major international financial institutions – the World Bank, the IMF, the regional development banks, and increasingly, the membership of the World Trade Organization – have

made explicit that they will be accountable for achieving the Goals too.

⇨ The world has never before seen so much prosperity. The hundreds of billions that are being spent in Iraq have put things in perspective. We might not need more than about $50 billion of additional aid per year to meet the Goals. About $900 billion was invested in arms by governments in 2003 alone; and rich countries grant large support to their domestic agricultural producers, totalling $300 billion each year. Financially, in the grand scheme of things, we're talking about relatively small change.

If we carry on in a 'business as usual' mode, the Goals will not be achieved by 2015

⇨ Performance against the goals is being monitored. These are not just lofty statements of intent; precise monitoring mechanisms have been put in place, in the form of national Millennium Goals reports and the Secretary General's reports to the General Assembly. Civil society organisations around the world are creating their own set of reports as well, to ensure that governments are held to the highest possible standards of performance. Over 60 country reports have already been produced at the national level.

⇨ The Goals are clearly achievable. Some have even argued that they are not in fact millennium, but 'minimum' development goals. We believe that to set the bar any lower than this would be morally unacceptable. Individual Goals have already been achieved by many countries in the space of only 10-15 years.

⇨ The above information is reprinted with kind permission from the UN Millennium Campaign. Visit www.endpoverty2015.org for more information.

© UN Millennium Campaign

Fast facts: environmental sustainability

Information from the United Nations Population Fund

⇨ More than 1 billion people lack clean water and more than 2.6 billion live without adequate sanitation.

⇨ Some 60 per cent of the world's poor live in fragile and highly vulnerable areas on arid and semi-arid lands, on steep slopes and in forests.

⇨ Long-term poverty reduction and sustainable growth can be undermined by the degradation of the natural resource base, scarcity and lack of access to water, and air pollution, which affect health and livelihoods.

⇨ Population growth, along with high resource consumption by affluent populations, is contributing to increasing stress on the global environment.

⇨ The bulk of future population growth will occur in the developing regions of the world least able to absorb it. Slowing and stabilising population growth gives countries time to take steps that meet people's needs yet protect the environment.

⇨ Natural resources are conserved when individuals have the information and services they need to plan smaller, healthier families.

⇨ The 20 per cent of the world's people living in the highest-income countries are responsible for 86 per cent of total private consumption, compared with the poorest 20 per cent, who account for only 1.3 per cent of consumption.

⇨ Women grow a substantial portion of the world's food, and there is considerable evidence that their labour-intensive food production practices tend to be environmentally sound.

⇨ Appropriate and integrated social, population and sustainable development policies and programmes that empower the poorest people, especially women, will support a sustainable future.

⇨ The above information is reprinted with kind permission from the United Nations Population Fund. Visit www.unfpa.org for more information or to view references.

© United Nations Population Fund

What is sustainable development?

Information from Sustainable Development

The past 20 years have seen a growing realisation that the current model of development is unsustainable. In other words, we are living beyond our means. From the loss of biodiversity with the felling of rainforests or over-fishing to the negative effect our consumption patterns are having on the environment and the climate. Our way of life is placing an increasing burden on the planet.

The increasing stress we put on resources and environmental systems such as water, land and air cannot go on for ever. Especially as the world's population continues to increase and we already see a world where over a billion people live on less than a dollar a day.

A widely-used and accepted international definition of sustainable development is: *'development which meets the needs of the present without compromising the ability of future generations to meet their own needs'* – globally we are not even meeting the needs of the present let alone considering the needs of future generations.

Unless we start to make real progress toward reconciling these contradictions we face a future that is less certain and less secure. We need to make a decisive move toward more sustainable development. Not just because it is the right thing to do, but also because it is in our own long-term best interests. It offers the best hope for the future. Whether at school, in the home or at work, we all have a part to play. Our small everyday actions add up to make a big difference.

Guiding principles of sustainable development

The UK Government, Scottish Executive, Welsh Assembly Government and the Northern Ireland Administration have agreed upon a set of principles that provide a basis for sustainable development policy in the UK. For a policy to be sustainable, it must respect all five principles, outlined in the box below.

UK priorities

In terms of focusing our efforts, the UK has identified four priority areas for immediate action, shared across the UK, these are:

⇨ Sustainable consumption and production;
⇨ Climate change and energy;
⇨ Natural resource protection and environmental enhancement;
⇨ Sustainable communities.

The UK Government also recognises that changing behaviour is a cross-cutting theme closely linked to all of these priorities. In addition, *Securing the Future* identifies well-being as being at the heart of sustainable development.

The principles and approaches are covered in more detail in *Securing the Future – the UK Government's sustainable development strategy* and the *UK Strategic Framework*.

⇨ Visit www.sustainable-development.gov.uk for more information.

© Crown copyright

Shared UK principles of sustainable development
As the UK Government, Scottish Executive, Welsh Assembly Government and the Northern Ireland Administration, we have agreed upon the following set of shared UK principles that will help us to achieve our sustainable development purpose. They bring together and build on the various previously existing UK principles to set out an overarching approach, which our four separate strategies can share.

Living within environmental limits
Respecting the limits of the planet's environment, resources and biodiversity – to improve our environment and ensure that the natural resources needed for life are unimpaired and remain so for future generations.

Achieving a sustainable economy
Building a strong, stable and sustainable economy which provides prosperity and opportunities for all, and in which environmental and social costs fall on those who impose them (Polluter Pays), and efficient resource use is incentivised.

Ensuring a strong, healthy and just society
Meeting the diverse needs of all people in existing and future communities, promoting personal well-being, social cohesion and inclusion, and creating equal opportunity for all.

Using sound science responsibly
Ensuring policy is developed and implemented on the basis of strong scientific evidence, whilst taking into account scientific uncertainty (through the Precautionary Principle) as well as public attitudes and values.

Promoting good governance
Actively promoting effective, participative systems of governance in all levels of society – engaging people's creativity, energy, and diversity.

The UK's ecological debt

'China-dependence' going up for life in UK, as world as a whole goes ever further into 'ecological debt'

For 2007, from Saturday 6 October, the world as a whole went into ecological debt driven by over-consumption. 'Ecological debt day' is the date when, in effect, humanity uses up the resources the earth has available for that year, and begins eating into its stock of natural resources. World ecological debt day has crept ever earlier in the year since humanity first began living beyond its environmental means in the 1980s. The latest available data reveals that the overuse of the earth's resources is much more extreme in rich countries. For example, if everyone in the world wanted to live like people in the UK, on a very conservative estimate, we would need more than three planets like Earth.

> **'Ecological debt day' is the date when, in effect, humanity uses up the resources the earth has available for the year, and begins eating into its stock of natural resources**

This was just one of the findings of a new report from nef, *Chinadependence: the second UK Interdependence report*, published in association with the Open University. Released on the day that the world as a whole went into ecological debt for 2007 – marked internationally by the Global Footprint Network – *Chinadependence* reveals the many ways in which Britain is becoming increasingly dependent on the rest of the world to fuel our high-consuming lifestyles. In particular, *Chinadependence* reveals a striking rise in the UK's dependence on a wide range of Chinese imports.

economics as if people and the planet mattered

And, because the greenhouse gas pollution that results from their manufacture is blamed on China, not the consumers in the UK, in effect we are turning China into our 'environmental laundry' with devastating consequences for the planet.

Chinadependence also reveals that Britain's dependence on the rest of the world for basics like food and energy is still rising. The report, the second overview of the UK's place in the international system by nef, shows that the burden in terms of resource consumption that our lifestyles exert on the fields, forests, rivers, seas and mines of the rest of the world is still increasing despite increased public concern about climate change. This comes as other research shows that a high quality of life is as easy to achieve at very low levels of consumption as at high levels, and as awareness is growing that the pursuit of high-consuming lifestyles undermines well-being.

'During the recent banking emergency people feared that the UK would slide from a liquidity crisis into an insolvency crisis. Few saw the link between easy credit and over-consumption that is leading to a far worse problem: an environmental insolvency crisis. This report shows the urgent need to develop a sensible and positive pattern of interdependence between the UK, the rest of the world and the earth's life-support systems,' says Andrew Simms, lead author of the report and nef policy director.

'As the world creeps closer to

irreversible global warming and goes deeper into ecological debt, why on earth, say, would the UK export 20 tonnes of mineral water to Australia, and then re-import 21 tonnes? And why would that wasteful trade be more the rule, than the exception. In the face of collective challenges like global warming, it makes clear that the UK's patterns of interdependence will have to change if our economy is to become remotely sustainable.'

'Our twentieth-century politics of short-termism and self-interest leave us lost in the face of climate change and the downsides of globalisation. This report helps us see the long threads of connection – ecological, cultural, and economic – that span our interdependent world. In doing so it writes a new map of our urgent political responsibilities,' adds Joe Smith, of the Open University, co-ordinator of the Interdependence Day project and report contributor.

Ecologically wasteful trade with the world as a whole is still rife in the UK economy

The report reveals that the UK is drifting into ever greater 'Chinadependence'. We are ever more clothing ourselves, furnishing our homes, watching television, listening to music, playing games with our children and even decorating our Christmas trees, courtesy of goods manufactured in China. For example:

➪ In the last year alone, our spending on imports from China rose 18 per cent to £15.6 billion and, more important environmentally, imports rose 10 per cent by weight to a total of just under 6.5 million tonnes.

➪ Over the past five years, our spending on, and the weight of imports have risen by over 125 per cent and 114 per cent respectively.

➪ In 2006, we imported 60,000 tonnes just of Christmas decorations.

China has become the 'environmental laundry' for the Western world. China is increasingly blamed for its levels of pollution in general, and its rising greenhouse gas emissions in particular. But it is demand from countries like the UK which leads to smoke from Chinese factories and power plants entering the atmosphere. Because China's energy mix is more fossil-fuel intensive than those of Europe, Japan or the USA, it also means that outsourcing to China creates more greenhouse gas emissions for each product made.

'As China is increasingly attacked because of its rising pollution levels, people overlook two important issues. First, per person, China's greenhouse gas emissions are a fraction of those in Europe and the United States. Second, a closer look at trade flows reveals that a large share of China's rising emissions is due to the dependence of the rest of the world on exports from China – a Chinadependence,' adds lead author and nef policy director, Andrew Simms.

'There is also the fact that a lot of heavy industry has simply relocated to China from apparently cleaner, richer nations – when our major retailers scour the world for the cheapest production costs, the result is that more greenhouse gases get pumped into the atmosphere for every product we buy. Because of the way that data on carbon emissions gets collected at the international level, this has the effect of "carbon laundering" economies like those of Britain and the USA,' he concludes.

The report also shows that ecologically wasteful trade with the world as a whole is still rife in the UK economy. Amongst several examples of economic and environmental inefficiency the report reveals that in 2006 alone:

➪ From all trading partners in total, the UK imported 14,000 tonnes of chocolate-covered waffles, and exported 15,000 tonnes.

➪ We both imported from and exported to Italy, 600 tonnes of 'gums and other jelly confectionery'.

➪ We sent 21 tonnes of mineral water all the way to Australia and brought 20 tonnes all the way back.

➪ The large, two-way traffic of beer between Spain and the UK is also almost identical in amount.

The report shows that the UK's growing interdependence with the rest of the world is both a fact and an opportunity. But, the report says, we are currently abusing it – by living so far beyond our environmental means and running up ecological debts we deny millions who go without, the chances for a better life and we put the planet's life support mechanisms in peril. Amongst other trends, the report reveals that Britain's dependence on basics like food and energy is still rising, and shows an economy increasingly dependent on international trade:

➪ The UK's ability to feed itself is still declining: for all food, the UK's self-sufficiency is now 27 per cent lower than it was in 1990, and has dropped seven per cent since 2002. Continuing a trend begun in the early-to-mid 1990s, the UK's self-sufficiency in providing food continues to fall. Even allowing for changes in the way the Government calculates its figures, our ability to feed ourselves, without depending on imports from overseas, is at its lowest ebb for half a century.

➪ The UK is less able to meet its own energy needs: since losing self-sufficiency in 2004, our 'energy dependence' has increased almost fourfold. In 2004, the UK lost its status as an energy independent nation. Since then we have relied on imports to balance supply and demand.

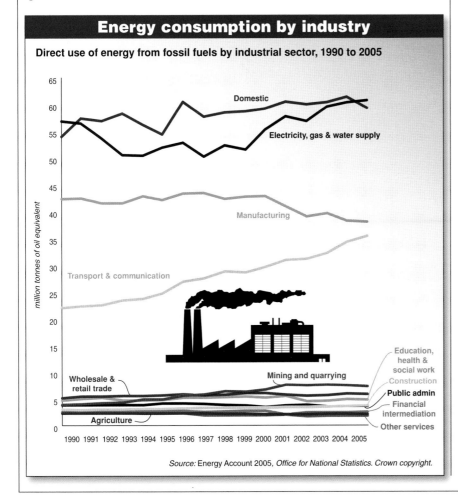

Energy consumption by industry

Direct use of energy from fossil fuels by industrial sector, 1990 to 2005

million tonnes of oil equivalent

Domestic

Electricity, gas & water supply

Manufacturing

Transport & communication

Wholesale & retail trade

Mining and quarrying

Education, health & social work

Construction

Public admin

Financial intermediation

Agriculture

Other services

1990 1991 1992 1993 1994 1995 1996 1997 1998 1999 2000 2001 2002 2003 2004 2005

Source: Energy Account 2005, *Office for National Statistics. Crown copyright.*

Even though the country has huge untapped renewable energy sources, including some of the best supplies of potential wind energy in Europe, our dependence on energy imports is increasing.

⇨ Britain's dependence on international trade is increasing despite rising fuel prices and fears about climate change: International trade makes up a growing share of the UK's income. Trade as a share of GDP is at its highest point for over four decades and on an upward trend.

⇨ There is also a human price to be paid by the rest of the world for our lifestyles. We are still highly reliant on overseas workers to staff our schools and hospitals draining some of the world's poorest counties of vital human resources. And, the report reveals, increases in overseas aid have been dwarfed by money from developing countries deposited in UK banks.

⇨ The UK still relies on health workers from poor countries: as issues of immigration refuse to leave the mainstream political debate, the reality appears to be that many of our vital public services could not function without the arrival of skilled professionals from overseas. In the last five years alone, the UK has imported 289 trained nurses from Malawi, 364 from Botswana and 757 from Zambia. South Africa, Ghana, Kenya, Lesotho and Zimbabwe also send nurses trained in the health systems of Africa to work in the NHS. The popular myth of the UK being a soft touch for health tourists masks a reality in which we are being tended in our sick beds by nurses that many poor countries can ill afford to lose.

⇨ UK: important aid donor or haven for money on the run? According to figures from the Bank of England, in 2006, money from developing countries deposited in UK banks surged by over $124 billion – around $10 billion more than in 2005 – lifting total deposits to $514 billion. In 2006, nef revealed that

in spite of the UK Government's commitment to increasing its aid budget, another barely noticed trend, the rise in money from developing nations deposited in UK banks, cast questions over the nation's financial role in relation to developing countries. Overall, a range of factors will be influential but, generally, the removal of controls over the movement of money around the world, and 'capital flight' are both likely factors.

Chinadependence reveals how the nation is being woven into an ever closer and more complicated international economic, cultural and social fabric, with both positive and negative consequences.

A positive future, the report suggests, will only be guaranteed through a paradigm shift in government policy away from 'beggar-thy-neighbour' economic competitiveness, towards the cooperation demanded by our inescapable interdependence. As a minimum commitment to positive global interdependence, the report calls on the UK Government to:

⇨ Adopt the ecological footprint as an official measure, with a timetable, policies and resources to move the UK to live within its fair, per capita share of available global biocapacity – so-called 'one planet living'.

⇨ Commit to reversing the decline in the UK's food self-sufficiency alongside a published timetable.

⇨ Commit to year-on-year greenhouse gas emissions reductions

in line with a minimum cut of 80 per cent by the year 2050. This could be achieved by following the road map to an 80 per cent cut in UK emissions by 2050 set out by Craig Simmons, technical director of Best Foot Forward.

⇨ Commit to greater energy security and independence by introducing significant measures for demand reduction, increased efficiency, deployment of renewable energy technologies and the introduction of more efficient, mini and medium-scale grids for distribution.

⇨ Take action to prevent the UK being a haven for dubious capital flight from developing countries.

⇨ Compensate developing countries where a brain and skills drain of publicly trained professionals – such as from health services across Africa – benefits the UK.

⇨ Celebrate the public enrichment that comes from living in a society comprised of many cultures that is part of an interdependent world. And, as part of that, to publicly acknowledge the day in the year when, in effect, the UK stops depending on its own means, and begins to live off the rest of the world.

6 October 2007

⇨ This extract is reprinted with kind permission from nef (the new economics foundation). The full text can be downloaded at www.neweconomics.org

Sustainable consumption and production

To live within our resources, we need to achieve more with less. This requires us to change the way we design, produce, use and dispose of the products and services we own and consume

The problem with the way we produce and consume goods

Today we live in both a carbon constrained and water constrained world. Pressures on the environment are increasing as world population grows and parts of society become wealthier. The planet's renewable resources – like water, timber or fish – are rapidly being exhausted and our use and disposal of non-renewable resources are radically altering our environment.

The extent to which we are using resources, including the 'sinks' we rely on to deal with the waste we produce, means that the chances of developing countries – and future generations – to have access to their fair share of resources are threatened.

Our own wellbeing and quality of life, as well as the health of ecosystems, are becoming increasingly compromised by pollution and over-exploitation of resources. A situation created, in large part, by our enormous, collective consumer appetite.

A new way of doing business

Current production practices and consumption levels are the source of many of the environmental challenges we face, requiring us to urgently develop products and services using fewer resources and to prevent waste. This will certainly mean using cleaner technologies, but it will also require new ideas to encourage us to meet our needs in different, less harmful ways. Today, we need to innovate to redesign products, rethink business models and restructure systems.

While Government has an important role to play in stimulating companies to act through incentives, rewards and the threat of penalties, it is ultimately businesses that will deliver a supply of goods and services

that are less damaging and more resource efficient. We need to reach a situation where companies regard environmental care as important as customer care.

Forward-thinking companies are already seeing the opportunities that this presents and the benefits it can have to the bottom line by driving down costs, opening up markets through innovation, and enhancing reputations and brand value.

How to develop better products and services

People need to be able to choose to live more sustainable lifestyles. However, in many instances, consumers are denied any real choice as many of the avoidable impacts of what we use and buy are already 'designed in' long before they reach consumers.

Some innovative producers are using eco-design tools to rethink products and services; creating goods that perform as well or better than conventional products, using resources more productively, reducing pollution and improving profitability.

How to improve resource efficiency

With rising energy and waste costs, tougher environmental legislation and higher stakeholder expectations, organisations are increasingly focusing their attention on improving production practices to both enhance performance and demonstrate responsible behaviour.

Improved resource productivity has the potential to drive down costs by reducing raw material use, waste and pollution. The penalties for failing to manage environmental risks properly can also be substantial, whether in terms of lost reputation, loss of the licence to operate, build or market, or straight financial penalties.

How to encourage sustainable consumption

Current consumption patterns similar to those of the UK could not be replicated worldwide. Some calculations suggest that this would require three planets' worth of resources. Instead we need to move towards 'one planet living'.

There is huge potential for better products and production practices to deliver improvements without the need for behaviour change on the part of consumers. However, a sustainable society will require that all sectors – businesses, public sector and households – consume differently and more efficiently.

How to develop a responsible business

Many businesses have realised that acting in a socially and environmentally responsible manner is more than just an ethical duty for a company. It is something that affects the bottom line.

Sustainable development is an area of risk that, when managed effectively, can create opportunities. Companies can make financial savings on energy costs, reduced inputs, waste disposal and compliance with regulations. They can enhance reputation and brand value, fostering customer loyalty and motivating staff. Companies can also use it as an opportunity to encourage innovation, increase investment and open up new markets.

Updated 11 September 2006

⇨ The above information is reprinted with kind permission from Sustainable Development. Visit www.sustainable-development.gov.uk for more information about sustainability and the environment.

© Crown copyright

Securing the future

An extract from the Government's *Sustainable Development Strategy*

Our strategy for sustainable development aims to enable all people throughout the world to satisfy their basic needs and enjoy a better quality of life without compromising the quality of life of future generations.

The UK is on track to meet its Kyoto target – a significant achievement

Chapter 1: A new strategy

The Government has a new purpose and principles for sustainable development and new shared priorities agreed across the UK, including the Devolved Administrations. The strategy contains:

⇨ a new integrated vision building on the 1999 strategy – with stronger international and societal dimensions;

⇨ five principles – with a more explicit focus on environmental limits;

⇨ four agreed priorities – sustainable consumption and production, climate change, natural resource protection and sustainable communities, and

⇨ a new indicator set, which is more outcome focused, with commitments to look at new indicators such as on wellbeing.

Chapter 2: Helping people make better choices

We all – governments, businesses, public sector, voluntary and community organisations, communities and families – need to make different choices if we are to achieve the vision of sustainable development.

The Government proposes a new approach to influencing behaviours based on recent research on what determines current patterns. The Government will focus on measures to enable and encourage behaviour change, measures to engage people, and ways in which the Government can lead by example. Where these are not sufficient to change entrenched habits, we will also look for ways to catalyse changes.

Chapter 3: 'One planet economy' – sustainable consumption and production

Increasing prosperity, in the UK and across the world, has allowed many people to enjoy the benefits of goods and services which were once available to just a few. We have also made progress in cleaning up some of the worst industrial pollution. Nevertheless, the environmental impacts of our consumption and production patterns remain severe, and inefficient use of resources is a drag on the UK economy and businesses. In addition, internationally we need to promote the mutual supportiveness of trade liberalisation, environmental protection and sustainable development to help developing countries.

We need a major shift to deliver new products and services with lower environmental impacts across their lifecycle, and new business models which meet this challenge while boosting competitiveness.

And we need to build on people's growing awareness of social and environmental concerns, and the importance of their roles as citizens and consumers.

Chapter 4: Confronting the greatest threat – climate change and energy

The UK Government is committed to reducing the country's greenhouse gas emissions. In its 2003 Energy White Paper, the Government put the goal of moving to a low carbon economy at the heart of its energy strategy, and set out a long-term goal of reducing carbon dioxide emissions by some 60 per cent by about 2050, with real progress to be shown by 2020.

In addition, we have a target under the Kyoto Protocol to reduce greenhouse gas emissions by 12.5 per cent below base year levels by 2008-12, and a more ambitious national goal of reducing carbon dioxide emissions by 20 per cent below 1990 levels by 2010. Our Climate Change Programme sets out policies and measures to help achieve these goals.

The UK is on track to meet its Kyoto target – a significant achievement. However, more needs to be done to achieve our national 2010 goal. Through the current

review of the UK Climate Change Programme the Government is committed to evaluating the existing programme measures and aims to publish a revised programme in summer 2005.

Chapter 5: A future without regrets – protecting our natural resources and enhancing the environment

Natural resources are vital to our existence and to the development of communities throughout the world. The issues we face are the need for better understanding of environmental limits, the need for environmental enhancement where the environment is most degraded, the need to ensure a decent environment for everyone, and the need for a more integrated policy framework to deliver this.

Chapter 6: From local to global – creating sustainable communities and a fairer world

The Government will promote joined-up solutions to locally identified problems, working in partnership to tackle economic, social and environmental issues.

At the local level, we are announcing a package of measures to realise the vision of sustainable communities across England, in both urban and rural areas, which will catalyse the delivery of sustainable development.

At the national level, the strategy sets out the framework for changing people's lives through improvements in public services and providing opportunity for all.

At the global level, we look at how we will apply the principles of good governance, democracy and partnership and how to work effectively to meet locally identified priorities so that this country helps meet Millennium Development Goals.

⇨ The above information is reprinted with kind permission from Sustainable Development. Visit www. sustainable-development.gov.uk to view the Sustainable Development Strategy is full.

© Crown copyright

What are natural resources?

Information from Sustainable Development

Natural resources can be thought of in five overlapping ways. Each of these reflects values that we associate with them.

Raw materials such as minerals and biomass

Minerals, such as fossil fuels, metal ores, gypsum and clay, are non-renewable because they cannot be replenished within a human timescale. In contrast, biomass is in principle renewable within the human timeframe, and includes quickly renewable resources, like agricultural crops, and slowly renewable resources like timber. However, both of these can be pushed beyond their limits of recovery if over-exploited.

Flow resources such as wind, geothermal, tidal and solar energy

These resources cannot be depleted, but require other resources to exploit them. For example, energy, materials and space are needed to build wind turbines or solar cells.

Environmental media such as air, water and soil

These resources sustain life and support biological resources on which we depend.

Space is required to produce or sustain all the above

Space provides land for our cities and towns, infrastructure, industry and agriculture. It is also required by wildlife, rivers and natural processes for them to function healthily.

Biological resources include species and genetic information

Plants, animals and other organisms maintain the life-sustaining systems of the earth. Their variability (biodiversity) is also a resource and includes the diversity within species, between species and of ecosystems.

⇨ Information from Sustainable Development. Visit www. sustainable-development.gov.uk for more.

© Crown copyright

Ecological Footprint

Information from the Global Footprint Network

The Ecological Footprint is a resource management tool that measures how much land and water area a human population requires to produce the resources it consumes and to absorb its wastes under prevailing technology.

In order to live, we consume what nature offers. Every action impacts the planet's ecosystems. This is of little concern as long as human use of resources does not exceed what the Earth can renew. But are we taking more?

Today, humanity's Ecological Footprint is over 23% larger than what the planet can regenerate. In other words, it now takes more than one year and two months for the Earth to regenerate what we use in a single year. We maintain this overshoot by liquidating the planet's ecological resources. This is a vastly underestimated threat and one that is not adequately addressed.

By measuring the Ecological Footprint of a population (an individual, a city, a nation, or all of humanity) we can assess our overshoot, which helps us manage

Global Footprint Network
Advancing the Science of Sustainability

our ecological assets more carefully. Ecological Footprints enable people to take personal and collective actions in support of a world where humanity lives within the means of one planet.

The challenge and the goal: sustainability

Sustainability is a simple idea. It is based on the recognition that when resources are consumed faster than they are produced or renewed, the resource is depleted and eventually used up. In a sustainable world, society's demand on nature is in balance with nature's capacity to meet that demand.

When humanity's ecological resource demands exceed what nature can continually supply, we move into what is termed ecological overshoot. According to a report by the World Resources Institute, the United Nations Environment Programme, the United Nations Development Programme, and the World Bank, *World Resources 2000-2001, People and Ecosystems: The Fraying Web of Life*, in addition to the growing depletion of non-renewable resources such as minerals, ores and petroleum, it is increasingly evident that renewable resources, and the ecological services they provide, are at even greater risk. Examples include collapsing fisheries, carbon-induced climate change, species extinction, deforestation, and the loss of groundwater in much of the world.

Sustainability is a simple idea. It is based on the recognition that when resources are consumed faster than they are produced or renewed, the resource is depleted and eventually used up

---

We depend on these ecological assets to survive. Their depletion systematically undermines the well-being of people. Livelihoods disappear, resource conflicts emerge, land becomes barren, and resources become increasingly costly or unavailable. This depletion is exacerbated by the growth in human population as well as by changing lifestyles that are placing more demand on natural resources.

⇨ Source: Global Footprint Network 2006. National Footprint Accounts, 2006 Edition. Available at www.footprintnetwork.org

Sustainable construction

Information from the Environment Agency

The construction industry plays a major role in improving the quality of the built environment, but it also impacts on the wider environment in a number of ways.

The construction business in the UK is responsible for nearly a third of all industry-related pollution incidents. Construction and demolition waste alone represent 19% of total UK waste. Too many buildings are environmentally inefficient and do not make best use of limited resources such as energy and water. The energy used in constructing, occupying and operating buildings represents approximately 50% of greenhouse gas emissions in the UK.

The construction sector uses over 420 million tonnes of material resources

---

Sustainable construction techniques have been successfully used to deliver projects such as the Great Western Hospital in Swindon and the Millennium Village in Greenwich. Yet take-up of sustainability principles varies significantly, with some leading firms following recognised good practice, but others still making little effort. The environmental efficiency of buildings in the UK remains lower than in many other European countries. An increase in the number of single-person households, together with rising domestic waste production and water consumption, means that increases in environmental efficiency are needed just to limit the impact of existing buildings.

Promoting sustainable construction is difficult because of the industry's size and fragmentation. The industry provides a tenth of

the UK's gross domestic product and employs 1.4 million people in many types of business.

The rate of construction in the UK is set to increase. The Government's Sustainable Communities Plan seeks to accelerate the current house-building programme and increase the house-building target by about 200,000 on top of the 900,000 new homes planned between 1996 and 2016 in the South East. This new emphasis on growth represents an opportunity to shift development towards delivering more sustainable homes and construction.

Background

⇨ The construction sector uses over 420 million tonnes of material resources and converts 6,500 hectares of land from rural to urban use each year.

⇨ Approximately 13 million tonnes of construction and demolition waste is material delivered to sites but never used.

⇨ Annually, 90 million tonnes of construction and demolition waste is generated – the industry produces three times the waste produced by all UK households combined.

⇨ Construction and demolition is responsible for creating 21% of the hazardous waste in the UK.

⇨ About 10% of national energy consumption is used in the production and transport of construction products and materials, and the energy consumed in building services accounts for about half of the UK's emissions of carbon dioxide.

⇨ Climate change is making flood management an increasingly important factor in deciding where to locate new development. Presently, 1.85 million houses and 185,000 commercial properties are at risk from flooding, figures that are likely to increase under planned future development.

⇨ The above information is reprinted with kind permission from the Environment Agency. Visit www.environment-agency.gov.uk for more information.

© Environment Agency

Population, poverty and the environment

Information from the United Nations Population Fund

Environmental sustainability is essential to achieving the Millennium Development Goals, especially poverty reduction. Changes in population size, rate of growth and distribution have a far-reaching impact on the environment and on development prospects.

The largest population increases and the most fragile environmental conditions are usually found in poor countries, which typically have limited financial means and least adequate political and managerial resources to address the challenges. This threatens sustainable development and produces further deterioration in living standards and quality of life.

Environmental crises have the greatest impact on the poor in developing countries. Achieving the goals of the Programme of Action of the International Conference on Population and Development (ICPD), especially universal access to gender-sensitive and quality reproductive health services, will help to achieve a more favourable equation between population and available resources.

Environmental degradation takes many forms, but the elements of most immediate consequence to the world's population relate to land, air and water. The two most serious infrastructure deficiencies in both rural areas and cities are contaminated water supplies and polluted air.

In the rural environment, land fragmentation, eroded slopes and degraded soils are contributing to poverty, hunger and migration.

The unplanned rapid growth of cities, fed partly by migrants from rural areas, is creating intense pressure on local ecosystems and has, in some cases, overwhelmed environmental resources. Millions have settled in slums and shantytowns without adequate shelter and basic services, including clean water and sanitation.

Poverty and environmental stress

The majority of the rural poor have increasingly become clustered on low-potential land. This has resulted from a combination of factors that vary in importance from one country to another – land expropriation, demographic pressures, intergenerational land fragmentation, privatisation of common lands, and consolidation and expansion of commercial agriculture with reduced need for labour.

Demographic pressures, among others, continue to play an underlying role in the geographical, economic and social marginalisation of the poor in most countries where there is a high incidence of poverty. Because they have been pushed or squeezed out of high-potential land, the rural poor often have no choice but to overexploit the marginal resources available to them through low-input, low-productivity agricultural practices, such as overgrazing, soil-mining and deforestation, with consequent land degradation.

Food and water security

Food and water security are becoming increasingly critical issues in many developing countries, especially where poverty and environmental degradation are endemic. People remain undernourished due to poverty, political instability, economic inefficiency and social inequity.

Population growth is creating a demand for stepped-up food sufficiency. While world food production is projected to meet consumption demands for the next two decades, long-term forecasts indicate persistent and possibly worsening food insecurity in many countries, especially in sub-Saharan

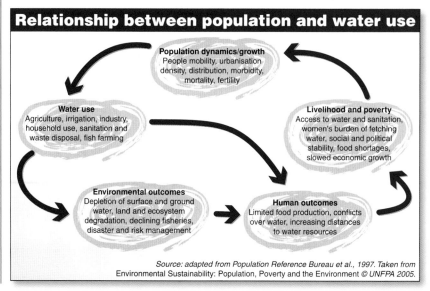

Relationship between population and water use

Population dynamics/growth
People mobility, urbanisation density, distribution, morbidity, mortality, fertility

Water use
Agriculture, irrigation, industry, household use, sanitation and waste disposal, fish farming

Livelihood and poverty
Access to water and sanitation, women's burden of fetching water, social and political stability, food shortages, slowed economic growth

Environmental outcomes
Depletion of surface and ground water, land and ecosystem degradation, declining fisheries, disaster and risk management

Human outcomes
Limited food production, conflicts over water, increasing distances to water resources

Source: adapted from Population Reference Bureau et al., 1997. Taken from Environmental Sustainability: Population, Poverty and the Environment © UNFPA 2005.

Africa. The Food and Agriculture Organization of the United Nations estimates that to meet the needs of the world's population in 2020, food production will have to double.

The Millennium Declaration target is to halve the proportion of people without access to safe drinking water and basic sanitation by 2015. It is estimated that more than 1 billion people lack clean water and more than 2.5 billion live without adequate sanitation. Many countries facing water scarcity are low-income societies with rapidly growing populations that are generally unable to make costly investments in water-saving technologies. Providing safe drinking water becomes a greater challenge as economic development and population growth place increasing demands on limited water resources.

Changes in population size, rate of growth and distribution have a far-reaching impact on the environment and on development prospects

In many less developed countries, increasing attention is being given to the critical role of women in population and environment programmes and in achieving sustainable development. Women make vital contributions to resource management and conservation. They provide food, fuel, fodder and water; are the caretakers of their family's health; and act as conservationists by safeguarding forests, soil, water and grazing areas. Women grow a substantial proportion of the world's food. Appropriate and integrated social, population and sustainable development policies and programmes that empower the poor, especially women, are needed to support a sustainable future.

⇨ The above information is reprinted with kind permission from the United Nations Population Fund. Visit www.unfpa.org for more information.
© United Nations Population Fund

The water crisis

Water crisis hits rich countries

Water crises, long seen as a problem of only the poorest, are increasingly affecting some of the world's wealthiest nations.

The report, *Rich countries, poor water*, is the most up-to-date overview of water issues in the developed world. It shows that a combination of climate change, drought and loss of wetlands, along with poorly thought-out water infrastructure and resource mismanagement, is creating a truly global crisis. It documents water problems beyond the situation in the UK, in other countries such as Australia, Spain, USA and Japan.

'Economic riches don't translate to plentiful water,' said Jamie Pittock, Director of WWF's Global Freshwater Programme. 'Water must be used more efficiently throughout the world – scarcity and pollution are becoming more common and responsibility for finding solutions rests with both rich and poor nations.'

Fresh water can no longer be considered to be a limitless resource. In Europe, countries along the Atlantic are suffering recurring droughts, while water-intensive tourism and irrigated agriculture are endangering water resources in the Mediterranean. In Australia, the world's driest continent, salinity is a major threat to a large proportion of its key agricultural areas.

Despite high rainfall in Japan, contamination of water supplies is a serious issue in many areas. In the United States, large areas are already using substantially more water than can be naturally replenished. This situation will only be exacerbated as climate change is predicted to bring lower rainfall, increased evaporation and changed snowmelt patterns.

Some of the world's thirstiest cities such as Houston and Sydney are using more water than can be replenished. It is notable that large cities with less severe water issues such as New York, with a population of eight million, tend to have a longer tradition of conserving areas important for water management such as catchment areas and expansive green areas within their boundaries.

Pittock continued: 'Regrettably, it appears that the next group of rapidly developing economies have already been seduced by major infrastructure plans, such as large dams, with inadequate consideration of whether such projects will meet water needs or inflict human and natural costs.'

In Brazil, despite leading the world with its national water resources plan, concerns remain over some existing dam proposals. In India much of its agriculture is under threat from rampant overexploitation of water resources. Elsewhere, China has raised international concerns over the scale and possible ecological and human costs of some of its massive water infrastructure plans.

'The crisis in rich nations is proof that wealth and infrastructure are no substitute for protecting rivers and wetlands, and restoring floodplain areas,' added Pittock.

The water problems affecting rich and poor alike are a wake-up call to return to protecting nature as the source of water. As we approach World Water Week governments must find solutions for both rich and poor, which include repairing ageing infrastructure, reducing contaminants, and changing irrigation practices in the way we grow crops.
16 August 2006

⇨ Information from the World Wildlife Fund. Visit www.wwf.uk for more information.
© World Wildlife Fund

2.6 billion wait in line for toilets

By Thalif Deen for the UN Millennium Campaign

There are more than 2.6 billion people, roughly 42 per cent of the world's population, waiting in line for toilets that just do not exist.

That's a reality, says the United Nations, which will launch the 'International Year of Sanitation', come November.

'No private toilets, no public toilets, no toilets anywhere,' chimes in the London-based non-governmental organisation End Water Poverty, following a survey of some of the world's poorest nations in Asia, Africa, Latin America and the Caribbean.

The organisation, whose global campaign calls for 'water and sanitation for all', declares: 'The international effort on sanitation and water is in disarray.'

Why do sanitation and water remain low priorities? 'A lack of political will to push through changes that benefit the poorest and the most vulnerable people in the world.'

The UN Children's Fund (UNICEF) points out that more than one billion people worldwide have gained access to improved sanitation over the past 14 years. Still, an estimated 2.6 billion people, including 980 million children, have lagged behind.

'Children are especially vulnerable to diseases caused by lack of proper sanitation,' says UNICEF executive director Ann Veneman. 'Poor sanitation and hygiene and unsafe water claim the lives of an estimated over 1.5 million children under the age of five every year.'

At any one time, half of the world's hospital beds are occupied by patients suffering from water-borne diseases, according to the Geneva-based World Health Organisation (WHO).

And in sub-Saharan Africa, a baby's chance of dying from diarrhoea is almost 520 times that of a baby born in Europe or the United States.

At the World Water Week conference in the Swedish capital, Anders Berntell, executive director of the Stockholm International Water Institute, cited WHO statistics indicating that in 38 of the 46 African countries more children under the age of five die from diarrhoea than HIV/AIDS.

'Still, HIV/AIDS gets much more attention internationally than diarrhoea, caused by inadequate sanitation and lacking hygiene,' he added.

'Access to sanitation is a fundamental issue of human dignity and human rights'

Berntell said, 'We still don't manage to get this message across, and I think we need to turn to ourselves, to critically analyse how we can improve in getting acceptance for what we know are facts.'

In a publication titled *Water for Life Decade, 2005-2015*, the United Nations has reinforced the grim facts and statistics relating to water and sanitation.

'Lack of safe water and adequate sanitation is the world's single largest cause of illness,' it says, and 'can spread such diseases as diarrhoea, cholera, dysentery, typhoid, hepatitis, polio, trachoma and tapeworms – many of which can be fatal to people in the developing world.'

And there are other water-associated diseases, such as malaria and filariasis, that affect vast populations worldwide. Malaria alone kills more than one million people every year.

The UN warns that increased urbanisation is also placing an enormous strain on existing water and sanitation infrastructure.

'Urban centres in developing countries have grown rapidly without adequate infrastructure planning, resulting in million of immigrants who have little access to safe sanitation or water supplies. This puts the entire population at risk, causing serious environmental damage.'

Among a laundry list of 'what needs to be done', the world body is calling for increased investments in sanitation infrastructure such as latrines and toilets in homes and in every school.

The UN is also calling for the participation of women in the planning and designing of water and sanitation facilities – looking at both issues from gender perspectives.

Other recommendations include: programmes on water, sanitation and hygiene education in every school; effective and sustained advocacy on water, sanitation and hygiene at all levels; and making water and sanitation a priority in disaster-response planning.

Anticipating a crisis, the 192-member UN General Assembly decided in 2006 to designate 2008 the 'International Year of Sanitation', to begin in November.

To coincide with the launch, the World Toilet Association in South Korea is holding an international conference, 21-25 November, to focus specifically on the global shortage of toilets and sanitary facilities.

Sim Jae-Duck, a member of the South Korean National Assembly and chairman of the organising committee for the upcoming Seoul conference, told IPS that an 'appalling 40 per cent of the world population is living without toilets or proper sanitation, causing enormous losses of human life due to the spread of disease'.

It is unfortunate, he said, that there is yet no international organisation specifically interested in problems relating to sanitation.

'We plan to set up such an organisation,' he said, perhaps with the collaboration of several countries that are expected to participate in the conference, including China, Japan, Russia, Britain, United States, Brazil, Turkey and South Africa.

UN Secretary-General Ban Ki-moon is confident that the International Year of Sanitation will shift the focus onto one of the most neglected health issues of our times: the lack of proper sanitation.

'Let us make this a remarkable year of global sanitation achievement, one that generates real, positive changes for the millions, or even billions of people, who do not yet enjoy this basic ingredient of human welfare,' he told a preparatory meeting in May.

'Access to sanitation is a fundamental issue of human dignity and human rights, and also of economic development and environmental protection,' he argued.

Around the world, he said, 'about two out of every five of our fellow human beings lack access to sanitation services... This is simply unacceptable.'

16 August 2007

⇨ The above information is reprinted with kind permission from the UN Millennium Campaign. Visit www.endpoverty2015.org for more information.

© UN Millennium Campaign

Plumbing beats penicillin

By Jenny Hope

We live in an age of mind-boggling medical advance. But the most significant health breakthrough of all took place 150 years ago, according to a poll of doctors and the public.

Up against antibiotics, anaesthetic, vaccines and the understanding of DNA, the benefits of clean water and sewage disposal gained most votes from 11,000 doctors and members of the public

Sanitation was voted as the number one medical milestone of recent times.

Up against competition from such revolutionary developments as antibiotics, anaesthetic, vaccines and the understanding of DNA, the benefits of clean water and sewage disposal gained most votes from 11,000 doctors and members of the public questioned by the *British Medical Journal*.

The poll was staged to mark the relaunch of the magazine, which was first published in 1840, the date used as a starting point for qualification.

The frontrunner for doctors was anaesthesia, with the public voting for antibiotics. But when their votes were combined, sanitation moved ahead with 16 per cent of the total.

Experts said the public health revolution that started in the mid-19th century was responsible for saving more lives than many other medical advances. Poor sanitation in the Third World is still responsible for millions of deaths every year.

The award is perhaps ironic at a time when cleanliness in hospitals is under the microscope with the spread of superbugs like MRSA.

But public health was in a somewhat worse state in 1854 when British physician John Snow took the initiative which is credited with inspiring the development of a facility we all now take for granted.

Convinced water was the source of an outbreak of cholera in Soho, Central London – while accepted wisdom was that it was carried in the air – he removed the handle from a neighbourhood water pump. His action cured the outbreak, and led to the acceptance that sanitation was critical to public health.

The so-called 'Sanitary Revolution' followed, led by social reformer Edwin Chadwick, bringing piped domestic water supplies, sewers rinsed by water and better urban drainage.

⇨ This article first appeared in the *Daily Mail*, 18 January 2007.
© Associated Newspapers Ltd

Environmental migration

'Moving deckchairs on the *Titanic*'

Recent waves of economic migrants into Europe are likely to be dwarfed by future flows of environmental refugees from drought-hit regions such as north Africa, according to a new study from the Optimum Population Trust.

The Earth's capacity to absorb migrants displaced by climate change, population growth and the spread of deserts is coming up against 'key environmental limits', says the OPT. Europe, now becoming a prime overspill destination for people displaced by environmental and population pressures in sub-Saharan Africa, is already suffering severe droughts and soil erosion. Other countries in Africa are meanwhile beset by tensions resulting from loss of fertile land and population growth.

'The growing influx of migrants arriving from Africa via Senegal and the Canary Islands, running recently at 20,000 arrivals a month [*Correction: See notes at end*], has already prompted action at an EU level and is almost certainly a taste of the future,' the OPT adds. 'Recent waves of economic migration into the EU are likely to be dwarfed by future flows of environmental refugees.' It points to UN calculations that 135 million people globally are at risk of being displaced by desertification and that some 60 million people are expected to move from the desertified areas in sub-Saharan Africa towards northern Africa and Europe in the next 20 years.*

In Sudan, for instance, where nomads are in conflict with farmers over shrinking amounts of fertile land, the impact of displaced peoples is greatest on neighbouring Chad, already suffering serious ecological and population conflicts. 'Other continents will only be able to take desertification "refugees" at the cost, in most cases, of serious damage to their own environment,' the study says.

Rosamund McDougall, of the OPT's Advisory Council, said: 'The growing scarcity of water and fertile land, coupled with continuing population growth, have created a situation where just about the entire planet, and not just the developing world, is under strain. This year we have had droughts throughout southern and western Europe, and there are more in prospect – as well as warnings of blackouts and brownouts because of shortages of energy.'

Europe's 25 member states lose 250 million tonnes of soil a year to erosion

---

'It's our humanitarian duty to provide help and shelter for environmental refugees but we must also recognise that large-scale migration in these circumstances is, at best, like moving the deckchairs on the *Titanic* – it will just shift the problem from one place to another. At worst, it will hugely intensify it since much of the damage to the global environment is caused by high-impact consumption in the developed world – and migrants rapidly become high-impact consumers.**

'Real ways to reduce the strains on land and water must include making family planning much more widely available and recognising population growth for what it is – one of the main causes of environmental crisis.'

The OPT study, published ahead of the UN conference on climate change in Nairobi*** and in the wake of the Stern report on the costs of climate change, says that climate change and desertification pose a serious threat to global food security. An estimated six million hectares of productive land, an area almost half the size of England, are lost to desertification globally every year. Arable land per person declined from 0.32 hectares in 1961-63 to 0.21 hectares in 1997-99 and is expected to drop further to 0.16 hectares by 2030.* According to the Earth Policy Institute, this year's world grain harvest is projected to fall short of consumption for the sixth time in the last seven years. World stockpiles at the end of the crop year were projected to drop to 57 days of consumption, the shortest buffer since the 56-day low in 1972 that triggered a doubling of grain prices.

By the end of 2005 there were 20.8 million refugees and displaced people worldwide, up six per cent on the previous year, and by the end of the decade, according to a study by UN experts, as many as 50 million people could be escaping the effects of 'creeping environmental deterioration'.*

However, desertification and soil erosion are increasingly serious problems in the developed world, with 30 per cent of the US hit by desertification, a third of Spain at risk of turning into desert and large areas of southern Italy also affected. Europe's 25 member states lose 250 million tonnes of soil a year to erosion, roughly half a tonne per head of population. In the UK three million tonnes of soil are washed into river and drainage systems annually, from over 40 per cent of UK farmland officially categorised as being 'vulnerable' to soil erosion. ****

Rosamund McDougall said soil loss in Italy, caused by water erosion, salinisation and urbanisation, was turning large parts of the south and the Mediterranean coast, mainly Sicily, Sardinia, and Apulia, into arid land. 'But Italian mothers are helping to reduce environmental stress. With a fertility rate of 1.3 children, they're allowing the number of Italian urbanisers and climate changers to decrease to a more sustainable level.'

Global human population is projected by the UN to grow by 2.5 billion to 9.1 billion by 2050, the OPT points out. 'If the average worldwide total fertility rate (2.65 in 2000-05) could be reduced by just half a child per woman (to 2.15, just above the replacement rate of 2.1), world population would still reach 7.7 billion in 2050, but there would be 1.4 billion fewer climate changers and 1.4 billion fewer to feed.'

Notes

* Figures from UN sources, including United Nations Convention to Combat Desertification. Desertification is defined as 'land degradation in arid, semi-arid and dry sub-humid areas resulting from various factors, including climatic variations and human activities.' (UNCCD)

**An EU citizen's ecological footprint – a measure of global environmental impact – is more than four times greater than an African's, according to the *Living Planet Report 2006* (WWF), published in October. A Briton's footprint is nearly six times greater than a citizen of Sudan or Chad. The *Living Planet Report*, co-authored by the Institute of Zoology and the Global Footprint Network, calculated that in 2003 humanity's ecological footprint was 25 per cent larger than the planet's biological capacity.

*** The second meeting of the parties to the Kyoto Protocol, and the 12th session of the conference of the parties to the Climate Change Convention, will be held in Nairobi, Kenya, 6-17 November 2006.

****Figures from UN and European Soil and Water Protection (SOWAP) project.

Migrant arrivals figure: In January 2007 the EU said that the number of migrants from sub-Saharan Africa arriving on the Canary Islands had risen to 31,000 in 2006, six times more than in 2005. About half a million illegal immigrants are estimated to enter the EU each year.

2 November 2006

⇨ The above information is reprinted with kind permission from the Optimum Population Trust. For more information on this and other issues, please visit www.optimumpopulation.org

© *Optimum Population Trust*

Urban growth and sustainable use of space

An extract from the United Nations Population Fund's 2007 *State of the World Population* report

The space taken up by urban localities is increasing faster than the urban population itself. Between 2000 and 2030, the world's urban population is expected to increase by 72 per cent, while the built-up areas of cities of 100,000 people or more could increase by 175 per cent.

The land area occupied by cities is not in itself large, considering that it contains half the world's population. Recent estimates, based on satellite imagery, indicate that all urban sites (including green as well as built-up areas) cover only 2.8 per cent of the Earth's land area. This means that about 3.3 billion people occupy an area less than half the size of Australia.

However, most urban sites are critical parcels of land. Their increased rate of expansion, and where and how additional land is incorporated into the urban make-up, has significant social and environmental implications for future populations.

From a social standpoint, providing for the land and shelter needs of poor men and women promotes human rights. It is critical for poverty alleviation, sustainable livelihoods and the reduction of gender inequalities.

The territorial expansion of cities will also affect environmental outcomes. The conventional wisdom has been that the expansion of urban space is detrimental in itself. Since many cities are situated at the heart of rich agricultural areas or other lands rich in biodiversity, the extension of the urban perimeter evidently cuts further into available productive land and encroaches upon important ecosystems.

At the same time, however, there is increasing realisation that urban settlements are actually necessary for sustainability. The size of the land area appropriated for urban use is less important than the way cities expand: global urban expansion takes up much less land than activities that produce resources for consumption such as food, building materials or mining. It is also less than the yearly loss of natural lands to agricultural activities, forestry and grazing, or to erosion or salinisation.

Asked the defining questions – 'If the world's population were more dispersed, would it take up more valuable land or less? Would dispersion release prime agricultural land? Would it help avoid the invasion of fragile ecosystems?' – the answer, in most countries, would be 'No!' Density is potentially useful. With world population at 6.7 billion people in 2007 and growing at over 75 million a year, demographic concentration gives sustainability a better chance. The protection of rural ecosystems ultimately requires that population be concentrated in non-primary sector activities and densely populated areas.

The conclusion that using land for cities is potentially more efficient only heightens the need for careful and forward-looking policies, in light of the rapid doubling of the urban population in developing countries.

⇨ The above information is reprinted with kind permission from the United Nations Population Fund. Visit www.unfpa.org for more information.

© *United Nations Population Fund*

Sustaining life on earth

Extract of a report from the Convention on Biological Diversity

Biodiversity – the web of life

Biological diversity – or biodiversity – is the term given to the variety of life on Earth and the natural patterns it forms. The biodiversity we see today is the fruit of billions of years of evolution, shaped by natural processes and, increasingly, by the influence of humans. It forms the web of life of which we are an integral part and upon which we so fully depend.

This diversity is often understood in terms of the wide variety of plants, animals and microorganisms. So far, about 1.75 million species have been identified, mostly small creatures such as insects. Scientists reckon that there are actually about 13 million species, though estimates range from 3 to 100 million.

Biodiversity also includes genetic differences within each species – for example, between varieties of crops and breeds of livestock. Chromosomes, genes, and DNA – the building blocks of life – determine the uniqueness of each individual and each species.

Yet another aspect of biodiversity is the variety of ecosystems such as those that occur in deserts, forests, wetlands, mountains, lakes, rivers, and agricultural landscapes. In each ecosystem, living creatures, including humans, form a community, interacting with one another and with the air, water, and soil around them.

It is the combination of life forms and their interactions with each other and with the rest of the environment that has made Earth a uniquely habitable place for humans. Biodiversity provides a large number of goods and services that sustain our lives.

At the 1992 Earth Summit in Rio de Janeiro, world leaders agreed on a comprehensive strategy for 'sustainable development' – meeting our needs while ensuring that we leave a healthy and viable world for future generations. One of the key agreements adopted at Rio was the

Convention on Biological Diversity

Convention on Biological Diversity. This pact among the vast majority of the world's governments sets out commitments for maintaining the world's ecological underpinnings as we go about the business of economic development. The Convention establishes three main goals: the conservation of biological diversity, the sustainable use of its components, and the fair and equitable sharing of the benefits from the use of genetic resources.

We are changing life on earth

The rich tapestry of life on our planet is the outcome of over 3.5 billion years of evolutionary history. It has been shaped by forces such as changes in the planet's crust, ice ages, fire, and interaction among species. Now, it is increasingly being altered by humans. From the dawn of agriculture, some 10,000 years ago, through the Industrial Revolution of the past three centuries, we have reshaped our landscapes on an ever-larger and lasting scale. We have moved from hacking down trees with stone tools to literally moving mountains to mine the Earth's resources. Old ways of harvesting are being replaced by more intensive technologies, often without controls to prevent over-harvesting. For example, fisheries that have fed communities for centuries have been depleted in a few years by huge, sonar-guided ships using nets big enough to swallow a dozen jumbo jets at a time. By consuming ever more of nature's resources, we have gained more abundant food and better shelter, sanitation, and health care, but these gains are often accompanied by increasing environmental degradation that may be followed by declines in local

economies and the societies they supported.

In 1999, the world's population hit 6 billion. United Nations experts predict the world will have to find resources for a population of 9 billion people in 50 years. Yet our demands on the world's natural resources are growing even faster than our numbers: since 1950, the population has more than doubled, but the global economy has quintupled. And the benefits are not equally spread: most of the economic growth has occurred in a relatively few industrialised countries.

At the same time, our settlement patterns are changing our relationship with the environment. Nearly half the world's people live in towns and cities. For many people, nature seems remote from their everyday lives. More and more people associate food with stores, rather than with their natural source.

The value of biodiversity

Protecting biodiversity is in our self-interest. Biological resources are the pillars upon which we build civilisations. Nature's products support such diverse industries as agriculture, cosmetics, pharmaceuticals, pulp and paper, horticulture, construction and waste treatment. The loss of biodiversity threatens our food supplies, opportunities for recreation and tourism, and sources of wood, medicines and energy. It also interferes with essential ecological functions.

Our need for pieces of nature we once ignored is often important and unpredictable. Time after time we have rushed back to nature's cupboard for cures to illnesses or for infusions of tough genes from wild plants to save our crops from pest outbreaks. What's more, the vast array of interactions among the various components of biodiversity makes the planet habitable for all species, including humans. Our personal health, and the health of our economy and human society, depends on the continuous supply of various ecological services that would be extremely costly or impossible to replace. These natural services are so varied as to be almost infinite. For example, it would be impractical to replace, to any large extent, services such as pest control performed by various creatures feeding on one another, or pollination performed by insects and birds going about their everyday business.

'Goods and Services' provided by ecosystems include:
⇨ Provision of food, fuel and fibre;
⇨ Provision of shelter and building materials;
⇨ Purification of air and water;
⇨ Detoxification and decomposition of wastes;
⇨ Stabilisation and moderation of the Earth's climate;
⇨ Moderation of floods, droughts, temperature extremes and the forces of wind;
⇨ Generation and renewal of soil fertility, including nutrient cycling;
⇨ Pollination of plants, including many crops;
⇨ Control of pests and diseases;
⇨ Maintenance of genetic resources as key inputs to crop varieties and livestock breeds, medicines, and other products;
⇨ Cultural and aesthetic benefits;
⇨ Ability to adapt to change.

Biodiversity under threat

When most people think of the dangers besetting the natural world, they think of the threat to other creatures. Declines in the numbers of such charismatic animals as pandas, tigers, elephants, whales, and various species of birds, have drawn world attention to the problem of species at risk. Species have been disappearing at 50-100 times the natural rate, and this is predicted to rise dramatically. Based on current trends, an estimated 34,000 plant and 5,200 animal species – including one in eight of the world's bird species – face extinction. For thousands of years we have been developing a vast array of domesticated plants and animals important for food. But this treasure house is shrinking as modern commercial agriculture focuses on

relatively few crop varieties. And, about 30% of breeds of the main farm animal species are currently at high risk of extinction. While the loss of individual species catches our attention, it is the fragmentation, degradation, and outright loss of forests, wetlands, coral reefs, and other ecosystems that poses the gravest threat to biological diversity. Forests are home to much of the known terrestrial biodiversity, but about 45 per cent of the Earth's original forests are gone, cleared mostly during the past century. Despite some regrowth, the world's total forests are still shrinking rapidly, particularly in the tropics. Up to 10 per cent of coral reefs – among the richest ecosystems – have been destroyed, and one-third of the remainder face collapse over the next 10 to 20 years. Coastal mangroves, a vital nursery habitat for countless species, are also vulnerable, with half already gone.

The rainforests: disappearing fast

Global atmospheric changes, such as ozone depletion and climate change, only add to the stress. A thinner ozone layer lets more ultraviolet-B radiation reach the Earth's surface where it damages living tissue. Global warming is already changing habitats and the distribution of species. Scientists warn that even a one-degree increase in the average global temperature, if it comes rapidly, will push many

species over the brink. Our food production systems could also be seriously disrupted.

The loss of biodiversity often reduces the productivity of ecosystems, thereby shrinking nature's basket of goods and services, from which we constantly draw. It destabilises ecosystems, and weakens their ability to deal with natural disasters such as floods, droughts, and hurricanes, and with human-caused stresses, such as pollution and climate change. Already, we are spending huge sums in response to flood and storm damage exacerbated by deforestation; such damage is expected to increase due to global warming.

The reduction in biodiversity also hurts us in other ways. Our cultural identity is deeply rooted in our biological environment. Plants and animals are symbols of our world, preserved in flags, sculptures, and other images that define us and our societies. We draw inspiration just from looking at nature's beauty and power. While loss of species has always occurred as a natural phenomenon, the pace of extinction has accelerated dramatically as a result of human activity. Ecosystems are being fragmented or eliminated, and innumerable species are in decline or already extinct. We are creating the greatest extinction crisis since the natural disaster that wiped out the dinosaurs 65 million years ago. These extinctions are irreversible and, given our dependence on food crops, medicines and other biological resources, pose a threat to our own well-being. It is reckless if not downright dangerous to keep chipping away at our life support system. It is unethical to drive other forms of life to extinction, and thereby deprive present and future generations of options for their survival and development.

Can we save the world's ecosystems, and with them the species we value and the other millions of species, some of which may produce the foods and medicines of tomorrow? The answer will lie in our ability to bring our demands into line with nature's ability to produce what we need and to safely absorb what we throw away.

What are the next steps?

Economic development is essential to meeting human needs and to eliminating the poverty that affects so many people around the world. The sustainable use of nature is essential for the long-term success of development strategies. A major challenge for the 21st century will be making the conservation and sustainable use of biodiversity a compelling basis for development policies, business decisions, and consumer desires.

Biological diversity – or biodiversity – is the term given to the variety of life on Earth and the natural patterns it forms

---

Promoting the long term

The Convention has already accomplished a great deal on the road to sustainable development by transforming the international community's approach to biodiversity. This progress has been driven by the Convention's inherent strengths of near universal membership, a comprehensive and science-driven mandate, international financial support for national projects, world-class scientific and technological advice, and the political involvement of governments. It has brought together, for the first time, people with very different interests. It offers hope for the future by forging a new deal between governments, economic interests, environmentalists, indigenous peoples and local communities, and the concerned citizen.

However, many challenges still lie ahead. After a surge of interest in the wake of the Rio Summit, many observers are disappointed by the slow progress towards sustainable development during the 1990s. Attention to environmental problems was distracted by a series of economic crises, budget deficits, and local and regional conflicts. Despite the promise of Rio, economic growth without adequate environmental safeguards is still the rule rather than the exception.

Some of the major challenges to implementing the Convention on Biological Diversity and promoting sustainable development are:

⇨ Meeting the increasing demand for biological resources caused by population growth and increased consumption, while considering the long-term consequences of our actions.

⇨ Increasing our capacity to document and understand biodiversity, its value, and threats to it.

⇨ Building adequate expertise and experience in biodiversity planning.

⇨ Improving policies, legislation, guidelines, and fiscal measures for regulating the use of biodiversity.

⇨ Adopting incentives to promote more sustainable forms of biodiversity use.

⇨ Promoting trade rules and practices that foster sustainable use of biodiversity.

⇨ Strengthening coordination within governments, and between governments and stakeholders.

⇨ Securing adequate financial resources for conservation and sustainable use, from both national and international sources.

⇨ Making better use of technology.

⇨ Building political support for the changes necessary to ensure biodiversity conservation and sustainable use.

⇨ Improving education and public awareness about the value of biodiversity.

The Convention on Biological Diversity and its underlying concepts can be difficult to communicate to politicians and to the general public. Nearly a decade after the Convention first acknowledged the lack of information and knowledge regarding biological diversity, it remains an issue that few people understand. There is little public discussion of how to make sustainable use of biodiversity part of economic development. The greatest crunch in sustainable development decisions is the short- versus the long-term time frame. Sadly, it often still pays to exploit the environment now by harvesting as much as possible as fast as possible because economic rules do little to protect long-term interests.

Truly sustainable development requires countries to redefine their policies on land use, food, water, energy, employment, development, conservation, economics, and trade. Biodiversity protection and sustainable use requires the participation of ministries responsible for such areas as agriculture, forestry, fisheries, energy, tourism, trade and finance.

The challenge facing governments, businesses, and citizens is to forge transition strategies leading to long-term sustainable development. It means negotiating trade-offs even as people are clamouring for more land and businesses are pressing for concessions to expand their harvests. The longer we wait, the fewer options we will have.

What can I do about biodiversity?

While governments should play a leadership role, other sectors of society need to be actively involved. After all, it is the choices and actions of billions of individuals that will determine whether or not biodiversity is conserved and used sustainably.

In an era when economics is a dominant force in world affairs, it is more important than ever to have business willingly involved in environmental protection and the sustainable use of nature. Some companies have revenues far greater than those of entire countries, and their influence is immense. Fortunately, a growing number of companies have decided to apply the principles of sustainable development to their operations. For example, a number of forestry companies – often under intense pressure from environmental boycotts – have moved from clear-cutting to less destructive forms of timber harvesting. More and more companies have also found ways to make a profit while reducing their environmental impacts. They view sustainable development as ensuring long-term profitability and increased goodwill from their business partners, employees, and consumers. Local

communities play a key role since they are the true 'managers' of the ecosystems in which they live and, thus, have a major impact on them. Many projects have been successfully developed in recent years involving the participation of local communities in the sustainable management of biodiversity, often with the valuable assistance of NGOs and intergovernmental organisations.

It is the choices and actions of billions of individuals that will determine whether or not biodiversity is conserved and used sustainably

Finally, the ultimate decision-maker for biodiversity is the individual citizen. The small choices that individuals make add up to a large impact because it is personal consumption that drives development, which in turn uses and pollutes nature. By carefully choosing the products they buy and the government policies that they support, the general public can begin to steer the world towards sustainable development. Governments, companies, and others have a responsibility to lead and inform the public, but finally it is individual choices, made billions of times a day, that count the most.

⇨ The above information is reprinted with kind permission from the Convention on Biological Diversity. Visit www.cbd.int for more.
© Convention on Biological Diversity

Your natural heritage: why it matters

Information from Natural Scotland

We depend on the natural world for every aspect of our lives. All farm crops and animals have descended from wild organisms. Fruit crops rely on the insects that pollinate their flowers. We take food from the wild, like fish or venison. Fishermen with their nets and rods are simply harvesting the natural biodiversity of the oceans or rivers.

We depend on the natural world for every aspect of our lives

As well as providing food, biodiversity supports leisure activities and tourism and gives us building materials and resources for education, medicine and research. Natural organisms help break down and make harmless the waste we throw away.

We have a responsibility to protect and maintain nature's variety – for our health, enjoyment and wellbeing today and for the prosperity and enjoyment of future generations.

This responsibility has never been more important than it is today.

Biodiversity under threat

People have been a major force in shaping Scotland's landscape and biodiversity for thousands of years and our influence continues. Some of our activities have benefited biodiversity but many haven't. Over the past twenty-five years a large number of species have been declining and even disappearing in worrying numbers. Much of Scotland's vital biodiversity is under threat.

Climate change is one major factor threatening biodiversity. As the climate changes, some plants and animals will find it harder to survive in Scotland while others will move here from further south. As dates of flowering or maturing for insects change due to changes in the climate, other species that eat them may not be able to keep in step and this may threaten their survival.

Another major threat are 'invasive non-native species' – animals and plants that have been transported out of their natural range. They threaten species that live here in Scotland, like the native red which is being ousted by the grey squirrel. Once established, invasive species are very difficult and costly to control or eradicate. They are likely to become more of a problem with further globalisation, increased travel, and the effects of climate change.

But it's not all bad news. Significant improvements have occurred in the state of Scottish biodiversity over the last decade, as a result of the action by government, voluntary organisations, landowners and other individuals. For example, the loss of the otter in the lowlands has been reversed, the quality of our rivers and lochs has improved and there has been a significant shift to more sustainable forest management.

⇨ The above information is reprinted with kind permission from Natural Scotland. Visit www.itsourfuture.co.uk for more information.
© Natural Scotland

Contaminated land

Information from the Environment Agency

Past industrial activities have contaminated some of the land in England and Wales. This land may be a health risk to people's health and the environment unless it's cleaned up. Contaminated land can be reclaimed and redeveloped after it's been cleaned up.

What is contaminated land?

Contaminated land is land that has been polluted with harmful substances to the point where it now poses a serious risk to human health and the environment. Contamination can be on the surface or below it.

Contaminated land is land that has been polluted with harmful substances

---

People often confuse it with 'brownfield land'. Brownfield sites are land or premises that have previously been used or developed. They may also be vacant, or derelict. However, they are not necessarily contaminated. Greenfield land is land that has never been built on.

The Government has increased the pressure to redevelop brownfield sites by setting a target of 60% of new homes to be built on brownfield land. Because of a greater awareness of environmental issues, developers need to know whether a site is contaminated.

How is contaminated land regulated?

Contaminated land is regulated in two main ways:

Town and Country Planning Act
Contamination or the potential for contamination should be considered during the planning process. Local authorities can place conditions on planning permissions requiring that developers investigate contamination and, where it's found, clean it up to prevent harm.

The Environment Agency supports this process for those sites where there is water pollution or the potential for water to become polluted.

Contaminated land regime
The regime comes into effect if a site is not being redeveloped but is causing or has the potential to cause significant harm.

Once again, local authorities are the lead regulator and we support them by regulating 'special sites'.

How much contaminated land is there?

No one knows exactly how much contaminated land there is. We calculate that around 325,000 sites (300,000 ha) have had some form of current or previous use that could have led to contamination. We do not expect all these to be contaminated to the point where we need to take action.

Until they are investigated and assessed, however, we can only estimate the true extent of actual contamination. We have calculated that around 33,500 sites have been identified so far as contaminated to some extent, and that 21,000 sites have been treated, predominantly through the planning regime.

Under the contaminated land regime local authorities have a duty to inspect sites across England and Wales to identify contaminated land causing, or having the potential to cause, significant harm. The majority of contaminated land sites are relatively small.

The most common pollutants at the sites were metals and organic compounds. Twenty-five of these are 'special sites' which means they fit a particular description in the regulations, and we are taking action to clean them up.

The responsibility for identifying and treating contaminated land in England and Wales is split between local authorities and ourselves.

What causes contamination?

Most contamination problems are due to a lack of care over industrial and waste management. In the UK, large-scale man-made contamination started during the Industrial Revolution. Bad industrial practices and accidents released potentially harmful substances into the land, aquifers (underground water stores) and rivers. Oil refineries, railways, steel works, illegal landfill sites, petrol stations, gas works and accidental industrial spills may have all been sources of contamination in the past. Contamination can also come from historical activities dating back hundreds of years, such as spoil heaps from some Roman lead mines, and from naturally occurring substances. We can now regulate industry to minimise pollution, but the legacy of historical contamination remains.

What is being done about contaminated land?

The Government introduced the contaminated land regime, set out in Part IIA of the Environmental Protection Act 1990, in England on 1 April 2000, and on 1 July 2001 in Wales. Part IIA was introduced to identify and clean up contaminated land that poses unacceptable risks to human health or the environment. Statutory guidance advises the regulators on how to interpret the regulations.

Local authorities and the Environment Agency are joint regulators under the regime with local authorities taking the lead role.

Increasingly developers and landowners are playing a vital role in restoring the land, regardless of whether they caused the contamination in the first place.

⇨ Information from the Environment Agency. Visit www.environment-agency.gov.uk for more.

© *Environment Agency*

Britain: the 'dustbin of Europe'

Britain tops landfill league and wins 'Dustbin of Europe' award

New figures revealed today show that Britain is officially the 'dustbin of Europe' as it dumps more household waste into landfill than any other country in the European Union.

Research by the Local Government Association, a cross-party organisation which represents councils in England, shows that in the most recent year where figures are comparable to EU countries, households in the UK sent more than 22.6 million tonnes of rubbish to landfill. The figures also show that Britain sent the same amount of rubbish to landfill as the eighteen EU countries with the lowest landfill rates combined – despite having almost twice the population of the UK.

Council leaders will warn that an area the size of Warwick, which covers 109 square miles, is already taken up by landfill, and if the current trend continues it is estimated the country will run out of landfill space in less than nine years' time.

The countries with the highest amount of household rubbish thrown into landfill for the most recent comparable year (2005) are:
⇨ The UK which dumps around 22.6 million tonnes.
⇨ Italy which dumps around 17.6 million tonnes.
⇨ Spain which dumps around 14.2 million tonnes.
⇨ France which dumps around 12 million tonnes.
⇨ Poland which dumps around 8.6 million tonnes.

While the amount of rubbish being thrown into landfill by Britain has declined markedly over the previous twelve months, European countries have also been drastically cutting the amount they send to landfill, leaving Britain still at the top of the rubbish heap.

Research recently published by the Local Government Association revealed up to 40 per cent of a regular household shopping basket cannot be recycled.

Local government leaders will warn that unless bold reforms are made by householders, shops, businesses and manufacturers, recycling rates will not rise fast enough to meet the EU Landfill Directive and help tackle climate change and will hit the pockets of taxpayers.

Councils, and consequently the taxpayer, are facing fines of up to £150 per tonne of rubbish that is sent to be dumped into landfill sites. According to the National Audit Office, fines of up to £200 million could hit taxpayers for the failure to cut the amount that is thrown in landfills.

Cllr Paul Bettison, Chairman of the LGA Environment Board, said:

'Britain is the dustbin of Europe with more rubbish being thrown into landfill than any other country on the continent. For decades people have been used to being able to throw their rubbish away without worrying about the consequences. Those days are now over.

'There needs to be an urgent and radical overhaul of the way in which rubbish is thrown away. Local people, businesses and councils all have a vital role to play to protect our countryside before it becomes buried in a mountain of rubbish.

'An area the size of Warwick is already being used to dump Britain's rubbish and unless the ways of people and business change then the UK will run out of landfill space in less than nine years' time. Reducing waste will also help cut carbon emissions that contribute to climate change.

'Since 1997, local people, businesses and councils have worked tirelessly to boost recycling rates from seven per cent to twenty-seven per cent. However, there is still far more that needs to be done if the taxpayer is going to be able to avoid the landfill fines that the EU and central government will impose in the coming years.

'The "save-as-you-throw" powers should help to encourage people to take more responsibility for the way they throw their rubbish away. Councils want a power, not a duty, so authorities can decide what's best for their local areas. If councils introduce save-as-you-throw schemes, it will be to promote recycling, not to generate extra cash through an extra stealth tax.

'Councils are on the frontline in the fight against climate change and are working hard to reduce the amount of waste sent to landfill, but ultimately we must make sure less waste is produced in the first place.'
12 November 2007

⇨ The above information is reprinted with kind permission from the Local Government Association. Visit www.lga.gov.uk for more.
© *Crown copyright*

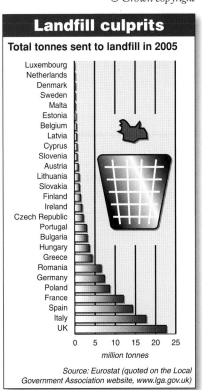

Landfill culprits

Total tonnes sent to landfill in 2005

Luxembourg
Netherlands
Denmark
Sweden
Malta
Estonia
Belgium
Latvia
Cyprus
Slovenia
Austria
Lithuania
Slovakia
Finland
Ireland
Czech Republic
Portugal
Bulgaria
Hungary
Greece
Romania
Germany
Poland
France
Spain
Italy
UK

0   5   10   15   20   25
million tonnes

Source: Eurostat (quoted on the Local Government Association website, www.lga.gov.uk)

Intrusion

Information from the Campaign to Protect Rural England

What is the problem?

Across England the character of countryside near and far, nationally or locally cherished, is threatened with the intrusion of new development. We have produced new maps which show that the area affected by new development stretches far beyond their actual 'footprint'. This shadow of urban growth or new roads or runways means that with 11% of England already urbanised, 50% is seriously disturbed by the sight, noise, and movement of development. Relatively small expansion of the urban area could intrude upon a whole lot of countryside, unless it is carefully located.

Relentless rate of loss

The new intrusion maps for 2007 show a remorseless loss of undisturbed countryside. From the 1960s to 1990s the total area of England disturbed by the noise and visual intrusion of roads, urban areas and major infrastructure rose from 26% to 41%. In the past 15 years alone another 9% has been blighted. At this rate of loss much of what remains could all but disappear in the next 80 years – within our children's lifetimes. The picture

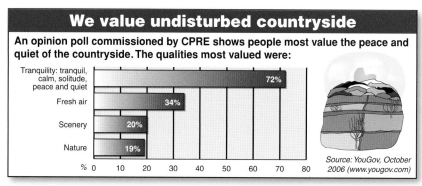

We value undisturbed countryside

An opinion poll commissioned by CPRE shows people most value the peace and quiet of the countryside. The qualities most valued were:

Tranquility: tranquil, calm, solitude, peace and quiet — 72%
Fresh air — 34%
Scenery — 20%
Nature — 19%
% 0 10 20 30 40 50 60 70 80

Source: YouGov, October 2006 (www.yougov.com)

varies from region to region. For instance, the South East, already growing beyond its capacity, is deeply fragmented with just 30% undisturbed countryside. The North East, the most tranquil region, still has 65% of its area undisturbed, yet has lost an area three times the size of Newcastle upon Tyne in just the past 15 years.

Why is this happening?

The pressures for development are constant. The planning system does its best to reconcile growth with the environment, but is often undermined. Countryside and the wildlife it shelters are not infinite, yet too often these are seen as expendable – to be traded off or 'balanced' against the need for new roads, jobs or homes. This 'balanc-ing act' leads to constant loss of land and intrusion into areas for miles around. But this loss and its wider effects are not inevitable. National government and regional and local planning authorities make the policies and decisions which change the countryside. They need to be smarter by steering development towards existing settlements, to find win-win solutions which enhance people's lives, the economy and the environment. If we lose the undisturbed countryside now, it is lost to us and to future generations.

⇨ The above information is reprinted with kind permission from the Campaign to Protect Rural England. Visit www.cpre.org.uk for more information.

© Campaign to Protect Rural England

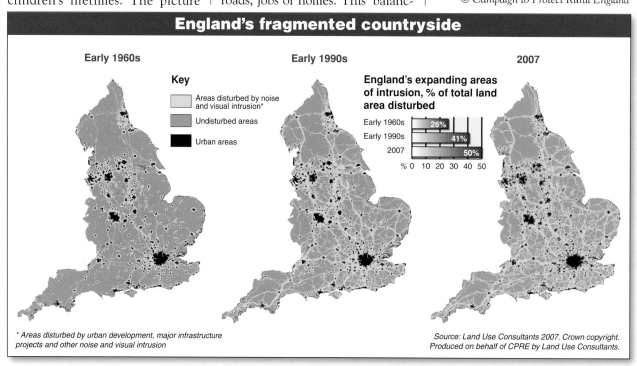

England's fragmented countryside

Early 1960s   Early 1990s   2007

Key
Areas disturbed by noise and visual intrusion*
Undisturbed areas
Urban areas

England's expanding areas of intrusion, % of total land area disturbed
Early 1960s — 26%
Early 1990s — 41%
2007 — 50%
% 0 10 20 30 40 50

* Areas disturbed by urban development, major infrastructure projects and other noise and visual intrusion

Source: Land Use Consultants 2007. Crown copyright. Produced on behalf of CPRE by Land Use Consultants.

Agricultural land use

Grassland and cereals dominate agricultural land in England and Wales, but the types of crops grown over the past 50 years have changed

How does agriculture affect the environment?

It is not farming but poor farm management that affects the environment. Agriculture accounted for over 5% of pollution incidents in 2005. Poor land management results in soil erosion, and fertiliser and pesticide run-off that can cause pollution. Good management can reduce these impacts.

Farming has changed the landscape and created new habitats that wildlife now depend on, such as field margins, woodlands, unimproved grasslands and hedgerows. Agri-environment schemes help to find ways in which habitats can be improved within farming systems. The area of land in agri-environment schemes in England has increased by 38 per cent to over one million hectares since 2000. It now accounts for about 12 per cent of the total agricultural area. By 2004 there were 2420 schemes participating in Tir Gofal, the Welsh whole farm agri-environment scheme, covering over a quarter of a million hectares.

From 2005 single farm subsidy payments to farmers under the Common Agricultural Policy (CAP) will depend on farmers achieving and maintaining baseline standards on environmental and public health, animal and plant health, and animal welfare.

Regional differences

Regional differences in land use reflect how the topography and climate are suited to different farming types. Arable crops dominate agricultural land use in the east of England. Grassland,

and hence grazing, dominates in the west and uplands.

The crop types grown also vary around the country. East Anglia and the East Midlands grow cereals in the greatest density. Fylde in Lancashire, Cornwall and the West Midlands have good growing conditions for vegetable crops. Potato production is widespread, but it is most common in East Anglia where the soil is good and the land is relatively flat.

⇨ The above information is reprinted with kind permission from the Environment Agency. Visit www.environment-agency.gov.uk for more.
© *Environment Agency*

Agricultural land use

Agricultural land use in England and Wales 2004

Legend:
- Arable
- Permanent grass
- Rough grazing
- Set aside
- Other

Area equivalent to 1000 thousand hectares
Area equivalent to 500 thousand hectares

North East
North West
Yorkshire and the Humber
East Midlands
Wales
West Midlands
East of England
South East
South West

Source: DEFRA. Crown copyright.

What is organic?

Information from the Soil Association

Organic systems recognise that our health is directly connected to the food we eat and, ultimately, the health of the soil.

Organic farmers aim to produce good food from a balanced living soil. Strict regulations, known as standards, define what they can and can't do. They place strong emphasis on protecting the environment.

Organic farmers use crop rotations to make the soil more fertile. For example, a farmer might graze sheep on a field one year, making the soil more fertile, then plant wheat the next and so on.

They can't grow genetically modified crops and can only use – as a last resort – seven of the hundreds of pesticides available to farmers.

Parasite problems in farm animals are controlled through regularly moving the animals to fresh pasture and other preventative methods, rather than routinely dosing the animals with drugs.

Here are some of organic farming's main features:

⇨ Organic farming severely restricts the use of artificial chemical fertilisers and pesticides.

⇨ Instead, organic farmers rely on developing a healthy, fertile soil and growing a mixture of crops.

⇨ Animals are reared without the routine use of drugs, antibiotics and wormers common in intensive livestock farming.

⇨ Information from the Soil Association. Visit www.soilassociation.org for more.
© *Soil Association*

Return of GM

Ministers back moves to grow crops in UK. Climate concerns will reduce chance of new public backlash, says industry

Government ministers have given their backing to a renewed campaign by farmers and industry to introduce genetically modified crops to the UK, the *Guardian* has learned.

They believe the public will now accept that the technology is vital to the development of higher-yield and hardier food for the world's increasing population and will help produce crops that can be used as biofuels in the fight against climate change.

'GM will come back to the UK; the question is how it comes back, not whether it's coming back,' said a senior government source.

Attempts to introduce GM to Britain in the late 1990s met a wave of direct action from activists tearing up crops. At the same time supermarkets such as Sainsbury's and Marks & Spencer barred GM ingredients from their ranges for fear of provoking a consumer backlash.

In 2004, the government announced that no GM crops would be grown in the country for the 'foreseeable future', prompting Lord Peter Melchett, policy director of the Soil Association, to declare: 'This is the end of GM in Britain.'

Recent polls also revealed that about 70% of the European public remained opposed to GM foods.

However, ministers are confident that the technology's virtues will be more apparent this time because of increased public awareness of pressing environmental concerns.

'The ability to have drought-resistant crops is important not only for the UK but for other parts of the world,' said the source. 'And the fact that some GM crops can produce higher yields in more difficult climatic conditions is going to be important if we're going to feed the growing world population.'

Ministers are reluctant to publicly back the effort at this stage, admitting that a previous attempt to introduce GM crops to the UK in 2004 fell

By Alok Jha
Science Correspondent

victim to poor public relations. 'We had a bad consultation on GM and it set research back in the UK a very long way indeed,' the source added.

Recent polls revealed that about 70% of the European public remained opposed to GM foods

In that year, scientists published the results of several field-scale trials of GM crops, which assessed their impact on the environment. Although the technology was subsequently cleared by the government, biotech companies in the UK decided to lie low after backlashes from the media, NGOs and consumers.

But industry attempts to reverse the situation are now gathering momentum. Earlier this year, the plant science company BASF began field trials in Cambridge and Yorkshire of a potato that has been genetically modified to resist blight, the fungus that devastated Ireland's potato crop and caused the famine of

the 1840s. A successful result could lead to the potato being the first in a line of GM crops grown in the UK.

'We have absolutely every confidence that GM will be used in the UK,' said Julian Little, chairman of the Agricultural Biotechnology Council, which represents several major biotechnology companies that produce GM crops.

'It's worth remembering that there are approximately 100m hectares (247m acres) of GM crops being grown around the world by about 10 million farmers. There is absolutely no question at all that this is technology that is being seen to work in other countries and why on earth would you not want to be interested in the UK?'

Farmers have been lobbying ministers over a way to bring back GM technology. Peter Kendall, the president of the National Farmers' Union (NFU), has written to ministers asking them to have a national debate to highlight the benefits.

Helen Ferrier, chief scientist at the NFU, said: 'We have written to ministers on various topics related to GM – including the more general issues of we've got to look at this more sensibly and try and have a conversation about it based on what's happening and not on emotions and what happened five years ago.'

SAME PRODUCT, NEW SPIN

Environment groups accused the government yesterday of putting industry wishes above the concerns of the public. 'Unfortunately the public and media have thought we've won the battle and GM's gone away and people aren't really worrying about it at the moment. It certainly hasn't gone away,' said Clare Oxborrow, a GM campaigner at Friends of the Earth.

Graham Thompson, of Greenpeace UK, said the government still saw GM as a public relations issue. 'The population has comprehensively rejected GM in the UK and over most of Europe so they're constantly having to be as bullish as possible. The purpose of the crops primarily is to give intellectual property rights to biotech companies. They're fulfilling their purpose perfectly in those terms. But they're not really doing much for the farmer.'

But Mr Little said environment campaigners had misled the public into fearing GM. 'All of the suggestions that they've made about the horrible things that could happen, nothing's happened.'

He pointed to Australia as a place where public opinion on GM technology was turned around. 'There's a country that has gone through the moratoriums, has gone through the we're-not-sure, the NGOs have been in there and caused mayhem, and come out the other end saying this is a useful technology and the public support it.'

'There is no question in our minds that we'll win,' said Mr Little. 'This is a safe, high-quality technology that's been proven to work.'

17 September 2007
© *Guardian Newspapers Limited 2007*

GM food: the solutions

Information from Greenpeace

The widespread introduction of genetically modified organisms (GMOs) poses enormous risks. Not enough research has been done into their impacts on other species or human health, and putting commercial gain for a few multinational corporations ahead of everything else is something we cannot afford to do.

The widespread introduction of genetically modified organisms (GMOs) poses enormous risks

We believe GMOs should not be released into the environment. Scientific understanding of their impact on plants, animals and human health is not adequate to ensure their safety.

We also oppose all patents on plants, animals and humans, as well as patents on their genes. Life is not an industrial commodity and when we force life forms and our world's food supply to conform to human economic models rather than their natural ones, we do so at our peril.

Sustainable agriculture

Instead, we advocate a move away from industrial-scale agriculture towards locally-focused and sustainable models. Feeding the world without exhausting the planet's natural resources is achievable, and it has to be a global priority – making sure everyone has enough to eat has to be more important than making money.

Study after study has shown the social and environmental benefits of sustainable and organic farming in both the affluent North and the impoverished South. These offer a practical way of restoring agricultural land degraded by the chemicals and over-production of industrial farming, allowing family farmers to fight poverty and hunger.

By championing organic, locally-produced food, we can challenge the threats posed by industrial agriculture and remove the flimsy arguments in favour of GM crops. Instead, we will have a farming system that works with nature, not against it.

⇨ The above information is reprinted with kind permission from Greenpeace. Visit www.greenpeace.org.uk for more.
© *Greenpeace*

Fisheries

Information from Seas At Risk

Over-fishing is widely acknowledged to be one of the major threats to marine biodiversity. Seas At Risk promotes sustainable fisheries management for the benefit of both fishers and the environment.

Currently 75% of global fish stocks are either fully exploited or over-fished, and according to the International Council for the Exploration of the Seas (ICES) the situation in the North East Atlantic is even worse. Over-fishing not only dramatically reduces fish stocks but the methods used also have devastating impacts on marine habitats and on non-target species such as dolphins and turtles; bottom trawling and by-catch are of particular concern. Over-fishing can even cause shifts in the balance of entire marine ecosystems through the large-scale removal of predatory fish and the current trend to 'fish down the food web'.

Deep water fisheries

As more traditional fish stocks have dwindled, fishers have moved into deeper waters in a 'gold rush' for new fisheries that has caused a rapid decline in stocks and left fisheries managers limping behind. Despite concern for the sustainability and long-term viability of deep water fisheries, there is at present no adequate monitoring, management or protection of these stocks. Seas At Risk promotes a precautionary approach to ensure sustainable deep water fisheries, both within EU waters and in the international waters of the North East Atlantic.

Deep water fish species tend to be slow growing, late maturing and low in reproductive capacity, which makes them particularly vulnerable to large-scale fishing activities. After a decade of ever stronger (but ignored) warnings, the International Council for Exploration of the Sea (ICES), the chief scientific advisory body on fisheries management in North East Atlantic waters, called in October 2005 for 'a complete overhaul of deep water fisheries'; with most deep water stocks at a historically low levels, ICES advise cutting back fishing as much as possible. In May 2006 they effectively repeated this same advice.

The two main regulatory bodies responsible for deep water fisheries' management in the North East Atlantic are the European Community (for all European waters) and the North East Atlantic Fisheries Commission (for international waters). Both have been ignoring scientific advice and their current deep water fisheries' management is totally inadequate. Seas At Risk is pushing for these two regulatory bodies to drop fishing effort to minimal levels until it can be shown to be sustainable, and to immediately introduce closed areas for the protection of spawning stocks and vulnerable habitats.

High seas bottom trawling

Bottom trawl fishing on the high seas is the most immediate and widespread threat to the unique and vulnerable biodiversity of the deep sea in international waters. For this reason Seas At Risk and many scientists, NGOs, and national authorities have been calling for the United Nations to establish a moratorium or temporary prohibition to provide protection for unique and largely unknown deep water areas of high biodiversity, e.g., seamounts, until effective and legally-binding measures can be put in place.

Because high seas bottom trawling is highly destructive, urgent protection measures are needed. Now is the time to take action, with the economic importance of this new fishery still relatively low. Most of the high seas beyond the 200nm Exclusive Economic Zones of coastal nations are unregulated. Against this background a UN General Assembly-declared moratorium on high seas bottom trawling is the only viable, short-term method of protecting deep sea ecosystems and fish stocks while a longer-term solution is agreed and implemented. Through our work with the Deep Sea Conservation Coalition (DSCC), a consortium of over 50 NGOs from around the world, this call is now supported by many nations around the world.

⇨ The above information is reprinted with kind permission from Seas At Risk. Visit www.seas-at-risk. org for more information.

© Seas At Risk

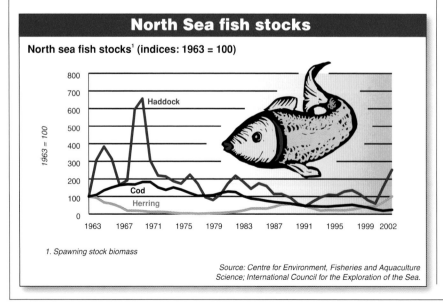

North Sea fish stocks

North sea fish stocks[1] (indices: 1963 = 100)

1963 = 100

Haddock

Cod

Herring

1963 1967 1971 1975 1979 1983 1987 1991 1995 1999 2002

1. Spawning stock biomass

Source: Centre for Environment, Fisheries and Aquaculture Science; International Council for the Exploration of the Sea.

Better buys: what fish can I eat?

If your supermarket, fishmonger or restaurant does not have a good policy on sourcing sustainable seafood, you will need to do the hard work yourself

Ask questions

Asking questions about your seafood sends a clear message to supermarkets and restaurants that people do care where their seafood comes from.

Is there something I haven't tried before?

Many stocks of the popular white fish such as cod or plaice are in bad shape – there may be plenty on the shelves, but there are not many left in the sea. Try something new – ask staff at the fish counter for a good alternative to your usual choice. Some supermarkets are promoting these alternatives each month – look out for these options. If consumers reduce consumption and broaden their tastes, then the pressure on popular species can be reduced.

What about oily fish such as mackerel, sardine or herring?

Stocks of these fish around the UK have improved, and they tend to be caught by less-destructive fishing methods.

Where is it from?

Choose seafood that has been sourced from small local UK fisheries. There are a number of reasons for this:

⇨ Local fishermen who are using or developing more sustainable methods need your support. Fish sourced from the waters of the south-west UK generally tend to be less depleted than those caught in the North Sea.

⇨ Climate change is already having a major impact on the marine environment – transporting seafood around the world is only adding to this problem.

⇨ Fish from the other side of the world may be taken from poorer communities that rely on fish as their main source of protein – you have many other choices.

How was it caught?

Choose line-caught fish wherever possible. Line-caught fish from small-scale fisheries don't have the bycatch or stock-depletion problems that are associated with trawling with massive nets. Line-caught fish also tend to be of better quality than trawled or netted fish. The line-caught sea bass and mackerel fisheries in SW England are a good option.

Not all lines are good, however. If you must eat tuna, then go for skipjack or yellowfin caught by rod-and-line. Avoid tuna caught by long-lines unless you are sure that the lines have been specially adapted to avoid catching threatened species such as seabirds, sharks and turtles.

For shellfish, choose hand-gathered scallops, winkles, clams, oysters or mussels rather than dredged ones, and pot-caught crabs, langoustines (scampi), and lobsters.

Be wary of farmed fish

Aquaculture is often promoted as being the solution to sustainable fisheries, and has undergone a massive growth over the last 50 years. Unfortunately, with the exception of some shellfish farms and freshwater fish reared in ponds, most aquaculture exacerbates the pressures placed on over-exploited marine ecosystems. In particular:

⇨ Wild caught fish are used for fishmeal and fish oil to feed farmed stocks. It takes over three tonnes of wild fish to produce one tonne of salmon.

⇨ Industrial fishing for smaller fish like sandeels and anchovies for use in fishmeal has caused massive disruption to marine food webs. It has almost certainly led to the decline in numbers of cod, seals and seabirds in the North Sea.

⇨ Disease spreads easily from farmed to wild populations, further depleting wild stocks.

⇨ Water and surrounding eco-systems are polluted by chemicals, antibiotics and vaccines used to control diseases in intensively farmed fish.

⇨ Many aquaculture practices are associated with poor human rights records, including loss of land and access to fishing grounds and poor employee rights.

Buy Organic- or Freedom Food-certified seafood

Fish or shellfish farms that have organic certification have the highest environmental standards in the aquaculture industry. The main organic certifier, the Soil Association, is raising its standards to ensure that any wild-caught fish used in farmed fish feed is minimised and sourced sustainably.

Freedom Food standards developed by the RSPCA for farmed fish are also good. Although the standards are primarily welfare-based, the better environment which they provide for the fish not only produces healthier fish, but also reduces the impact on the marine environment around the farm.

Buy herbivorous fish

Fish like carp, tilapia, and barramundi are herbivores – they eat plants and don't need to be fed with fishmeal. In the UK these fish tend to be farmed in enclosed ponds and have a lower impact on the surrounding environment.

⇨ The above information is reprinted with kind permission from Greenpeace. Visit www.greenpeace.org.uk for more information.

© Greenpeace

Forests

Information from Greenpeace

The problems

We are destroying ancient forests at an unprecedented rate. As demand for anything made from wood increases – whether it's books, furniture, construction materials or even toilet paper – we risk stripping away the last remaining ancient forest areas.

We are destroying ancient forests at an unprecedented rate. As demand for anything made from wood increases we risk stripping away the last remaining ancient forest areas

Extinction threatens many species, particularly larger animals such as tigers, grizzly bears and gorillas that need large intact forest areas to survive. In addition, the rights of traditional landowners are being abused as they are evicted from the lands they have occupied for generations, often as a result of violence and intimidation. Sixty million indigenous people depend on forests for their survival, while a further 1.6 billion make their livelihoods from forest products.

Destructive logging

More and more areas of pristine forest are being cut down to feed timber and paper mills around the world – an area the size of a football pitch disappears every two seconds. Much of this logging is destructive and can also be illegal, particularly in poorer countries where corruption, weak governance, and a lack of money make it difficult for the authorities to police and enforce the law.

GREENPEACE

Agriculture

Deforestation is also being driven by another human factor – agriculture. Ancient rainforests are being cleared to open up new land for crops such as soya and palm oil, which are grown on an industrial scale to supply the growing demand from food companies across the world, including the UK. The land is often stolen from the people who live there, and in the Amazon farms in cleared areas of forest still use slave labour.

Climate change

From storing carbon to recycling water into the atmosphere, it's increasingly clear that ancient forests play a critical role in the regulation of the global climate while their destruction is a major contributor to climate change. Deforestation accounts for 18 per cent of all emissions, more than the entire global transport sector, so protecting our ancient forests from further devastation is absolutely essential if we're serious about tackling climate change.

Failure of government and markets

If these threats are so apparent, why have governments not done more to combat them? Simply put, there is a distinct lack of political will on all sides to take action. In the developing world, a lack of funding for management and policing protected areas is aggravated by widespread corruption, while in industrialised nations products made from illegally logged timber

---

Ancient and semi-natural woodland

Ancient semi-natural woodland (ASNW) tends to be richer in plants and animals than other woodland areas. The area of ASNW has declined over the centuries and woodlands have become increasingly fragmented. In a 2001 report it was estimated to total 326 thousand hectares, of which almost two-thirds was in England. Later estimates, produced by overlaying the Ancient Woodland Inventory on the National Inventory of Woodland and Trees, give lower figures, but are not considered reliable.

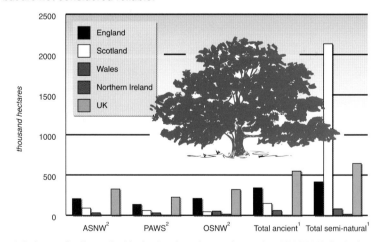

1. Ancient woodland is woodland that has been in continuous existence since 1600 (1750 in Scotland); Semi-natural woodland is woodland with natural characteristics (predominantly native species of trees, ground plants and animals).
2. ASNW (ancient semi-natural woodland) is both ancient and semi-natural; PAWS (plantation on an ancient woodland site) is ancient but not semi-natural; OSNW (other semi-natural woodland) is semi-natural but not ancient.

Source: Protected Forest Areas in the UK (S Pryor & G Peterken, 2001) with Northern Ireland data from Back on the Map (Woodland Trust, 2007). Quoted on the Forestry Commission website (www.forestresearch.gov.uk)

are cheaper than those produced in an environmentally and socially responsible way.

Even our own government can't abide by its own guidelines for buying timber – despite Tony Blair's verbal commitments towards forest protection, it's still absurdly easy to find products made from illegal and unsustainably logged timber on sale in this country.

The answers

Ancient forests around the world are at risk from a range of man-made threats including destructive and illegal logging, agriculture and climate change. Unchecked, these will destroy the last remaining forests, possibly within our lifetimes. But there are ways we can avert the crisis and preserve what remains of these fragile landscapes.

> **With only 8 per cent of the world's ancient forests currently under strict protection, huge areas are still at risk from destructive logging**

Protected areas

With only 8 per cent of the world's ancient forests currently under strict protection, huge areas are still at risk from destructive logging. So a global network of protected areas needs to be established to preserve the remaining intact ancient forest areas and the biodiversity they support. This won't happen overnight, so in the interim we need moratoria on all new industrial logging in these areas for either timber or agriculture while conservation plans are developed.

But creating protected areas won't happen without money in place to fund them. We need to make sure that when reserves are established, mechanisms for financing forest management and policing are in place which will prevent the logging companies from carrying on with business as usual.

Government action

Only governments can provide the legislation needed to establish protected areas, so we have to convince them that they need to take action. They also have the power to eliminate the trade in illegal and destructively-logged timber entering the UK and Europe by introducing legislation to stop illegal timber imports. Closing the markets for this kind of wood will send a clear signal to logging companies that their practices need to change before it's too late.

Changing industry

Companies and industry also have a significant role to play in forest protection and management. By using only timber and paper that comes from environmentally responsible and socially just forest management, they can have a huge impact on the rate of deforestation.

We've worked with a wide range of businesses to make this happen, and a range of companies – from timber merchants to building contractors, book publishers to paper manufacturers – are now taking action to ensure their businesses aren't contributing to the destruction of ancient forests. Unfortunately, many

other companies continue to conduct business as usual.

This isn't just limited to businesses dealing directly in timber products. With agriculture being a major cause of deforestation, food manufacturers and retailers also need to make sure their soya or palm oil is not being grown in newly deforested areas.

Certification schemes

Where logging does take place it needs to be environmentally responsible and socially just so that biodiversity is maintained and the forest is allowed to regenerate. Whilst there are many certification schemes on the market which claim to manage forests responsibly, in our opinion it's only the Forest Stewardship Council which can guarantee that timber products come from well-managed sources. This means trees are harvested in compliance with local laws, the forests are managed to a high standard, and that the rights of the local communities are respected.

⇨ The above information is reprinted with kind permission from Greenpeace. Visit www.greenpeace.org.uk for more information.
© Greenpeace

Conservation

Information from Natural England

Our objective is to conserve and enhance England's natural environment – including the landscape, biodiversity, geology and soils, natural resources, cultural heritage and other features of the built and natural environment.

Many areas of England are protected in National Parks, Areas of Outstanding Natural Beauty and other designated areas, and the condition of our very best wildlife sites is slowly improving. However, many of our landscapes are continuing to lose their ecological richness and their distinctive character.

The natural environment is a provider of a wide range of environmental services, including clean water and air, healthy food, recreation and inspiration. However, in many areas the natural environment is in poor condition, reducing the quality of these environmental services.

Ensuring that future generations can enjoy England's rich geology, landscapes and biodiversity means that we must significantly improve the protection and management of what we have today. Improving the condition of the natural environment is required to ensure that everyone benefits from the services it provides.

Designated areas

England's natural environment is unique and makes a major contribution to national and regional character. Our geology, soils, landscapes and their biodiversity along with our marine and coastal ecosystems are a rich inheritance.

National Nature Reserves

National Nature Reserves (NNRs) are some of the very finest sites in England for wildlife and geology, and provide great opportunities for people to experience nature. They have been established to protect and manage the special wildlife habitats, species and geological features that occur there. These features are of national and often international importance, and many NNRs are important for study and research. Almost all NNRs have some form of access provision – many are fully open throughout the year – as we want people to enjoy these wonderful places.

At present there is one Marine Nature Reserve (MNR) in England, which is Lundy Island in Devon.

At the end of September 2006, there were 222 reserves, covering over 92,000 hectares.

Local Nature Reserves

Local Nature Reserves (LNRs) are for both people and wildlife. They are living green spaces in towns, cities, villages and countryside which are important to people, and support a rich and vibrant variety of wildlife. They are places which have wildlife or geology of special local interest. All LNRs are owned or controlled by local authorities and some are also Sites of Special Scientific Interest.

At the end of July 2006 there were over 1,280 LNRs. Local Nature Reserves offer special opportunities for people to walk, talk, think, learn and play, or simply enjoy themselves. They make the places we live and work in more beautiful, healthier and less stressful.

Sites of Special Scientific Interest

Sites of Special Scientific Interest (SSSIs) are the country's very best wildlife and geological sites. There are over 4,000 SSSIs in England, covering around seven per cent of the country's land area. They include some of our most spectacular and beautiful habitats – wetlands teeming with waders and waterfowl, winding chalk rivers, gorse and heather-clad heathlands, flower-rich meadows, windswept shingle beaches and remote moorland and peat bogs. SSSIs support rare plants and animals that now find it difficult to survive in the wider countryside.

Over half of this SSSI land is also internationally important for its wildlife, and has been designated as Special Areas of Conservation (SACs), Special Protection Areas (SPAs) or Ramsar sites. Many SSSIs are also National Nature Reserves (NNRs) or Local Nature Reserves (LNRs).

National Parks

National Parks are extensive areas of land, each with their own managing authority to conserve and enhance their natural beauty, wildlife and cultural heritage and to promote opportunities for the understanding and enjoyment of their special qualities.

There are eight National Parks in England plus the Norfolk and Suffolk Broads, which have equivalent status. These nine areas account for eight per cent of England's land area.

National Parks provide their 110 million annual visitors with the opportunity to explore some of England's most dramatic and remote landscapes. The parks are living and working landscapes with an increasing focus on supporting the communities and economic activity which underpin their wild beauty.

Areas of Outstanding Natural Beauty

Areas of Outstanding Natural Beauty (AONBs) have been described as the jewels of the English landscape. There are 36 in all, covering about 15 per cent of England. The smallest is the Isles of Scilly, a mere 16 sq km, and the largest is the Cotswolds, totalling 2,038 sq km.

Natural England is responsible for designating AONBs and advising Government and others on how they should be protected and managed. Areas are designated solely for their landscape qualities for the purpose of conserving and enhancing their natural beauty.

Special Areas of Conservation

Special Areas of Conservation (SACs) are areas which have been given special protection under the European Union's Habitats Directive. They provide increased protection to a variety of wild animals, plants and habitats and are a vital part of global efforts to conserve the world's biodiversity.

England's SACs include areas which cover marine as well as terrestrial areas. Marine areas are not normally notified as Sites of Special Scientific Interest (SSSIs), except in intertidal areas and estuaries.

Heritage Coasts

England has many popular coastal resorts for those who enjoy the hustle and bustle of seaside towns. But 33% (1,057km) of scenic English coastline is conserved as Heritage Coasts.

These special coastlines are managed so that their natural beauty is conserved and, where appropriate, the accessibility for visitors is improved. The first Heritage Coast to be defined was the famous white chalk cliffs of Beachy Head in Sussex, the latest the Durham Coast. Now much of our coastline, like the sheer cliffs of Flamborough Head and Bempton, with their huge seabird colonies, is protected as part of our coastal heritage.

Wildlife

Biodiversity is the variety of life on the planet. This includes the plant and animal species that make up our wildlife – and the places or habitats in which they live. Natural England is responsible for ensuring that England's rich biodiversity is protected and improved.

The UK is one of 188 Parties to the Convention on Biological Diversity which was adopted at the Rio Earth Summit in 1992. This Convention has three main objectives: the conservation of biodiversity; the sustainable use of biodiversity; and the sharing of benefits from the use of genetic resources. In the UK this commitment led to the launch of the UK Biodiversity Action Plan (BAP) in 1994.

The Plan's overall goal is to conserve and enhance biodiversity

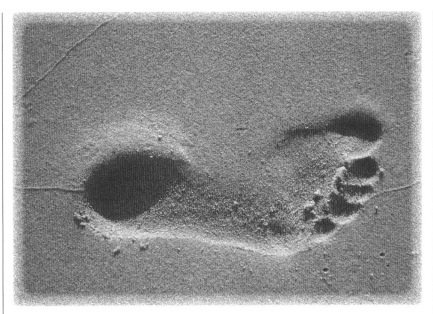

within the UK and to contribute to efforts to conserve global biodiversity. The UK BAP targets the recovery of some of our most threatened species and habitats in the terrestrial, freshwater and marine environments. For each priority species and habitat, an action plan describes the current status and threats, and sets out an action programme for achieving 10- to 15-year objectives and targets.

These action plans, and the UK BAP process as a whole, represent a consensus of Government, the statutory and voluntary conservation sectors, landowners and managers. They give us the best opportunity to date of reversing the major declines in the populations, range and quality of the UK's biodiversity resource.

Each of the four countries of the UK has subsequently produced country strategies for biodiversity. The England Biodiversity Strategy was published in 2003; it identified new approaches and partnerships across sectors as being essential for achieving the conservation of biodiversity.

At the Gothenburg Summit in 2001 the EU committed itself to the objective of halting the rate of biodiversity loss, with the aim of achieving this by 2010. At the World Summit on Sustainable Development in 2002, Heads of Government committed themselves to achieving a significant reduction in the rate of biodiversity loss by 2010. These, and other, multilateral environmental agreements cover the UK's action to conserve biodiversity both globally and within the UK.

Species Recovery Programme

Natural England's Species Recovery Programme seeks to reverse the declines in England's animals, plants and fungi. The programme recognises that current habitat-based management approaches are often not enough to prevent extinctions and restore species populations to a point where they are secure. Instead, targeted action is often required. This may include a dedicated research programme to understand why a species is declining and what its habitat needs are; a period of trial management to assess how best to reverse the decline (possibly requiring reintroductions); and a period of recovery management to increase population sizes. Natural England is involved in all stages of this recovery process.

Most of the species selected for our Species Recovery Programme are UK Biodiversity Action Plan priority species. We work in partnership with government, voluntary conservation organisations, landowners and business to deliver the targets for these species. Whenever possible, we also try to involve the public so that the enriched natural environments achieved by the Programme are enjoyed by all.

⇨ The above information is reprinted with kind permission from Natural England. Visit www.naturalengland.org.uk for more.
© Natural England

EU: top global importer of wildlife

Information from the World Wildlife Fund

The European Union tops the list for major importer of many wild animal and plant products, including tropical timber, caviar, reptile skins and live reptiles, according to a new report by TRAFFIC, the wildlife trade monitoring network.

The report, *Opportunity or threat: The role of the European Union in the global wildlife trade*, is the first ever analysis looking at the volume and scope of wildlife trade products imported into the EU.

'As EU membership has expanded, so has the size of the market and demand for wildlife products,' said Rob Parry-Jones, Head of TRAFFIC Europe.

'The demand for wildlife products in the EU is having a huge impact on wildlife and people in all corners of the world'

'While much wildlife trade is legal, we cannot ignore the growing illegal trade stemming from the demand for exotic pets, timber and other wildlife products. This is a serious threat to the survival of species such as reptiles and sturgeons.'

Between 2003 and 2004, EU enforcement authorities made over 7,000 seizures of shipments without legal permits, totalling over 3.5 million specimens listed under the Convention on International Trade in Endangered Species of Wild Fauna and Flora (CITES).

The legal trade of wildlife products into the EU alone was worth an estimated €93 billion in 2005. Wildlife products imported into the EU include caviar from the Caspian, snakeskin handbags and shoes, rare

WWF *for a living planet®*

reptiles as pets, as well as snooker cues made of ramin, a tropical hardwood tree from South-east Asia.

TRAFFIC estimates that from 2000 to 2005, 3.4 million lizards, 2.9 million crocodiles, and 3.4 million snake skins – all species listed under CITES – were imported into the EU, along with 300,000 live snakes for the pet trade.

During the same period, the EU imported 424 tonnes of sturgeon caviar – more than half of all global imports – and in 2004 alone, it imported more than 10 million cubic metres of tropical timber from Africa, South America and Asia, worth 1.2 billion.

According to WWF and TRAFFIC, well-regulated and legal trade can bring benefits to local people, local economies and conservation. For example, the EU imports 95 per cent of vicuña wool, providing significant income for 700,000 people in impoverished Andean communities. Vicuña is a wild relation of the llama that is sheared and its wool is exported under CITES rules from Bolivia, Peru, Argentina and Chile. Sustainable development of the vicuña wool trade has been supported by Italy, Germany and the European Commission.

'The demand for wildlife products in the EU is having a huge impact on wildlife and people in all corners of the world,' said Dr Susan Lieberman, Director of WWF's Global Species Programme. 'The EU has a key role in ensuring excessive demand does not cause over-exploitation

of wildlife outside its borders and a responsibility to help countries manage their resources.'

More than 170 governments will meet in the Netherlands from 3 to 15 June for the triennial CITES Conference of the Parties, the first ever to be held in the EU.

WWF and TRAFFIC believe the EU should lead the way in providing external assistance to countries where wildlife products originate and ensure their trade is sustainable.

Notes

⇨ TRAFFIC, the wildlife trade monitoring network, works to ensure that trade in wild plants and animals is not a threat to the conservation of nature. TRAFFIC is a joint programme of WWF and IUCN – The World Conservation Union.

⇨ CITES is an international agreement that regulates global wildlife trade. At this year's meeting, governments will discuss changes to the list of species protected under the convention, as well as other aspects of implementation of the treaty and controls on wildlife trade.

⇨ In December 2006, EU Environment Ministers formally acknowledged the need for EU assistance in promoting the conservation and sustainable use of wildlife in developing countries and effective implementation of the CITES Convention (Council Conclusions, 2773rd meeting of the Council of the European Union, 18 December 2006).

31 May 2007

⇨ The above information is reprinted with kind permission from the World Wildlife Fund. Visit www.wwf.org for more information.

© *WWF*

Air pollution

Information from the UK Air Quality Archive

In both developed and rapidly industrialising countries, the major historic air pollution problem has typically been high levels of smoke and sulphur dioxide arising from the combustion of sulphur-containing fossil fuels such as coal for domestic and industrial purpose.

The major threat to clean air is now posed by traffic emissions. Petrol and diesel-engined motor vehicles emit a wide variety of pollutants, principally carbon monoxide (CO), oxides of nitrogen (NOx), volatile organic compounds (VOCs) and particulates (PM_{10}), which have an increasing impact on urban air quality. In addition, photochemical reactions resulting from the action of sunlight on nitrogen dioxide (NO_2) and VOCs from vehicles leads to the formation of ozone, a secondary long-range pollutant, which impacts in rural areas often far from the original emission site.

Acid rain is another long-range pollutant influenced by vehicle NOx emissions.

In all except worst-case situations, industrial and domestic pollutant sources, together with their impact on air quality, tend to be steady-state or improving over time. However, traffic pollution problems are worsening world-wide. Below is an introduction to the principal pollutants produced by industrial, domestic and traffic sources.

Sulphur dioxide

Sulphur dioxide (SO_2) is produced when a material, or fuel, containing sulphur is burned. Globally, much of the sulphur dioxide in the atmosphere comes from natural sources, but in the UK the predominant source is power stations burning fossil fuels, principally coal and heavy oils. Widespread domestic use of coal can also lead to high local concentrations of SO_2.

Even moderate concentrations may result in a fall in lung function in asthmatics. Tightness in the chest and coughing occur at high levels, and lung function of asthmatics may be impaired to the extent that medical help is required. Sulphur dioxide pollution is considered more harmful when particulate and other pollution concentrations are high.

Nitrogen oxides

Nitric oxide (NO) is mainly derived from road transport emissions and other combustion processes such as the electricity supply industry. NO is not considered to be harmful to health. However, once released to the atmosphere, NO is usually very rapidly oxidised to nitrogen dioxide (NO_2), which is harmful to health. NO_2 and NO are both oxides of nitrogen and together are referred to as nitrogen oxides (NOx).

The major threat to clean air is now posed by traffic emissions

---

Nitrogen dioxide can irritate the lungs and lower resistance to respiratory infections such as influenza. Continued or frequent exposure to concentrations that are typically much higher than those normally found in the ambient air may cause increased incidence of acute respiratory illness in children.

Fine particles

Fine particles are composed of a wide range of materials arising from a variety of sources including:
⇨ combustion sources (mainly road traffic);
⇨ secondary particles, mainly sulphate and nitrate formed by chemical reactions in the atmosphere, and often transported from far across Europe;
⇨ coarse particles, suspended soils and dusts (e.g. from the Sahara), sea salt, biological particles and particles from construction work.

Fine particles can be carried deep into the lungs where they can cause inflammation and a worsening of the condition of people with heart and lung diseases. In addition, they may carry surface-absorbed carcinogenic compounds into the lungs.

Ozone and volatile organic compounds

Ozone (O_3) is not emitted directly from any man-made source in any significant quantities. In the lower atmosphere, O_3 is primarily formed by a complicated series of chemical reactions initiated by sunlight. These reactions can be summarised as the sunlight-initiated oxidation of volatile organic compounds (VOCs) in the presence of nitrogen oxides (NOx). The sources of VOCs are similar to those described for NOx above, but also include other activities such as solvent use, and petrol distribution and handling.

The chemical reactions do not take place instantaneously, but can take hours or days, therefore ozone measured at a particular location may have arisen from VOC and NOx emissions many hundreds or even thousands of miles away. Maximum concentrations, therefore, generally occur downwind of the source areas of the precursor pollutant emissions. Ozone irritates the airways of the lungs, increasing the symptoms of those suffering from asthma and lung diseases.

Toxic organic micro-pollutants (TOMPs)

TOMPs are produced by the incomplete combustion of fuels. They comprise a complex range of chemicals some of which, although they are emitted in very small quantities, are highly toxic or carcinogenic. Compounds in this category include:
⇨ PAHs (PolyAromatic Hydrocarbons);
⇨ PCBs (PolyChlorinated Biphenyls);
⇨ Dioxins;
⇨ Furans;

TOMPs can cause a wide range of effects, from cancer to reduced immunity to nervous system disorders and interfere with child development. There is no 'threshold' dose – the tiniest amount can cause damage.

Benzene

Benzene is a volatile organic compound which is a minor constituent of petrol. The main sources of benzene in the atmosphere in Europe are the distribution and combustion of petrol. Of these, combustion by petrol vehicles is the single biggest source (70% of total emissions).

Possible chronic health effects include cancer, central nervous system disorders, liver and kidney damage, reproductive disorders, and birth defects.

1,3-butadiene

1,3-butadiene, like benzene, is a volatile organic compound emitted into the atmosphere principally from fuel combustion of petrol and diesel vehicles. 1,3-butadiene is also an important chemical in certain industrial processes, particularly the manufacture of synthetic rubber.

Possible chronic health effects include cancer, central nervous system disorders, liver and kidney damage, reproductive disorders, and birth defects.

Carbon monoxide

Carbon monoxide (CO) is a colourless, odourless poisonous gas produced by incomplete, or inefficient, combustion of fuel. It is predominantly produced by road transport, in particular petrol-engine vehicles.

This gas prevents the normal transport of oxygen by the blood. This can lead to a significant reduction in the supply of oxygen to the heart, particularly in people suffering from heart disease.

Lead and heavy metals

Since the introduction of unleaded petrol in the UK there has been a significant reduction in urban lead levels. In recent years industry, in particular secondary non-ferrous metal smelters, have become the most significant contributors to emissions of lead. The highest concentrations of lead and heavy metals are now therefore found around these installations in industrial areas.

Even small amounts of lead can be harmful, especially to infants and young children. In addition, lead taken in by the mother can interfere with the health of the unborn child. Exposure has also been linked to impaired mental function, visual-motor performance and neurological damage in children, and memory and attention span.

⇨ The above information is reprinted with kind permission from the UK Air Quality Archive, and was sourced from data produced by AEAT technology on behalf of DEFRA. Visit www.airquality.co.uk for more information.

© UK Air Quality Archive

Pollution putting groundwater supplies at risk, warns agency

By Ian Sample, Science Correspondent

Water drawn from ancient aquifers across Britain is steadily becoming unusable because of widespread pollution from fertilisers, pesticides, oil and other contaminants.

The warning appears in an Environment Agency report to be published tomorrow and follows countrywide testing of 7,300 groundwater supplies, which in some regions provide up to a third of available tapwater.

The report – *Underground, Under Threat* – highlights widespread leaks and chemicals spread on to farmland, known as diffuse pollution, as the greatest threat to groundwater, and estimates 81% of sites in England and 35% in Wales are at risk of failing water quality standards.

Poor water quality has already led to the closure of 146 groundwater sources in the past 30 years, leading to the loss of at least 425,000 cubic metres of water every day, enough to supply nearly 3 million people. But growing urbanisation and rising pollution are putting the supplies at even greater risk, the report claims.

Previous tests found pesticide contamination in more than a quarter of groundwater sites. The latest tests also revealed problems with nitrate contamination from fertilisers and traces of drugs such as the anti-bacterial triclosan, that might kill off microbes that help break down pollutants. Other chemicals, such as fuels, fuel additives and solvents, were also detected, but are too modern to know what their effects will be, the report adds.

'Groundwater is very vulnerable to pollution and while it takes just a few careless moments to pollute or contaminate, it can take decades or even centuries to recover. That's why we need to do what we can to stop it from being polluted in the first place,' said Tricia Henton, environment protection director at the Environment Agency.

18 October 2006

© Guardian Newspapers Ltd 2006

Why monitor air pollution?

Information from the London Air Quality Network

The purchase and operation of accurate and comprehensive air quality monitoring equipment is costly, so why spend this money on monitoring rather than improving air quality?

Many laws now require government and local authorities to ensure that air pollution does not exceed certain legal limits

Once emitted from exhausts or chimneys, the behaviour of air pollution is dictated by the weather. As the weather in this country is extremely variable, the behaviour of pollution is extremely variable. The situation is complicated further by atmospheric chemistry; pollutants react with other gases in the atmosphere and deposit onto surfaces such as roads and buildings. At present, our scientific understanding of air pollution is not sufficient to be able to accurately predict air quality at all times throughout the country. This is where monitoring can be used to fill the gap in understanding.

Monitoring provides raw measurements of air pollutant concentrations, which can then be analysed and interpreted. This information can then be applied in many ways.

Analysis of monitoring data allows us to assess how bad air pollution is from day to day, which areas are worse than others and whether levels are rising or falling. We can see how pollutants interact with each other and how they relate to traffic levels or industrial activity. By analysing the relationship between meteorology and air quality, we can predict which weather conditions will give rise to pollution episodes.

Another important use is in the validation of computer models.

Models are used to test 'what if' scenarios. For example, 'how much will air quality improve if traffic numbers reduce by 20%?' or 'what effect will building a power station near a certain town have?' The accuracy of these models can only be tested by comparison with actual monitoring data.

All of this information can then be used by the Government to make informed policy decisions. Environmental policy is constantly being updated in the light of scientific research.

Increased awareness in air quality issues has lead to the demand for more thorough and accessible information. Members of the public worried about pollution or with health problems worsened by pollution can benefit from such information. Up-to-date information taken from monitoring sites across the country can be broadcast to the public via television, teletext, dedicated help lines, or the Internet.

Many laws now require government and local authorities to ensure that air pollution does not exceed certain legal limits. EC law sets standards (known as Directives) for some pollutants and requires national governments to monitor air quality to show that the standards are not exceeded. The

Key points

⇨ Air pollution monitoring can help us understand how pollutants behave and their relationship with the weather.
⇨ Monitoring data can be used to validate pollution modelling, used to test 'what if' scenarios.
⇨ National and European law requires the monitoring of pollution levels. Results can be used to make informed policy decisions.
⇨ Members of the public benefit from easily available, accurate and up-to-date information on the quality of the air they breathe.

Government's National Air Quality Strategy makes it the responsibility of local authorities to use monitoring information to assess air quality in order to show that Air Quality Standards will not be exceeded in their area by certain deadlines.

⇨ The above information is reprinted with kind permission from the London Air Quality Network. Visit www.londonair.org.uk for more information.

© London Air Quality Network

Can shopping save the planet?

**The big high-street chains are falling over themselves to 'go green'.
But will any of it make any difference? Mark Lynas is far from convinced**

It isn't easy being green. You have to turn the thermostat down to a chilly 18°C in winter, spend ages taping up draughty windows, eat nothing but muddy parsnips all through February and wear charity shop cast-offs instead of proper clothes. Oh, the horror.

Not so fast, say today's big high-street chains. Now you can be green and gorgeous, eco-conscious and highly fashionable, simply by buying the latest climate-friendly consumer products. Never mind marching on Whitehall or Downing Street, or giving up flying: all you have to do to save the planet is shop. In today's fast-paced, mass-market society it's a tantalising vision – a march towards a low-carbon economy led by high-street spending power and requiring no great change in our affluent consumerist lifestyles. But can it happen?

Marks & Spencer certainly thinks so. Perhaps the leader in the corporate ethical revolution, M&S has launched Plan A (as in: there's no Plan B), a £200m eco-refit being rolled out across the entire company. It includes becoming carbon neutral by 2012 (equivalent, it claims, to taking 100,000 cars off the road every year), putting warning labels on air-freighted food produce, opening several model 'green' stores, reducing waste eventually to zero and converting key clothing ranges to 100% fairtrade cotton.

M&S is not alone. In recent months a green tidal wave has washed down the high street, with retailers falling over themselves to chase the climate-friendly pound, and to buff up their corporate PR credentials in the process. Just last week, Sir Terry Leahy, the chief executive of Tesco, said he was prepared to raise prices in his stores to deliver 'a revolution in green consumption'. Barclaycard,

meanwhile, has launched its new Breathe credit card, which promises to donate 50% of profits to projects that tackle climate change. The mobile-phone company O2 is offering special benefits for customers who hang on to their old handsets rather than upgrading when their contracts end. Sky is promoting itself as the environmental leader in the media field, and now purchases 100% renewable electricity to cover its operations.

In recent months a green tidal wave has washed down the high street

---

As if to emphasise that the battles of the past – between people and profit, the planet and corporate greed – are over, the Climate Group charity is calling its global warming business partnership 'We're in this Together'. We're all on the same side now, is the subtext. We all live on one planet. Hey, even corporate CEOs love their children. Why shouldn't they help lead us towards a solution to humanity's greatest-ever crisis?

As James Murdoch, widely credited with getting his father on side in the climate-change battle, wrote last year in the *Guardian*: 'Corporations should be involved in the climate-change debate. The issue cannot be simply left to governments or supranational bodies. But those of us who believe that climate change and the growth of CO_2 emissions are the biggest intergenerational issues the world faces need to take positive action.'

As if to emphasise its new role as an advocate on climate change, Sky has even added a 'carbon calculator' to its website, so punters can quickly work out their carbon footprints and get

tips on how to reduce them. Having already cut its own CO_2 emissions by 50% across all its operating sites, Sky now wants to do the same in people's living rooms, and is developing a set-top box with an automatic energy-saving standby function.

Most dramatically of all, Rupert Murdoch himself has pledged to use the whole of his News Corporation (which includes Sky, as well as a large slab of the world's media) to roll out climate-change messaging to all its viewers and readers. 'The climate problem will not be solved without mass participation by the general public in countries around the globe,' Murdoch says. 'And that's where we come in. Our audience's carbon footprint is 10,000 times bigger than ours. We want to inspire people to change their behaviour.'

However, you don't have to dig very deeply to start coming across some glaring contradictions in this new corporate crusade to save the world. If News Corporation really wants to inspire low-carbon behaviour among its audience, will it stop running car adverts and other enticements to carbon profligacy? The Sky Travel section of the company's website is stuffed with low-cost holiday and city-break offers, featuring destinations as far afield as the Dominican Republic and Egypt, with nary a mention of global warming. Much of News Corporation's US media network has been at the forefront of the climate denialist backlash, from the *New York Post* to Fox News. Will the big boss now send instructions for a change of tone, and force erring journalists to mug up on the science?

Indeed, the deeper you look, the more absurd this all gets. If O2 wants us to keep the same mobile phone handset for longer, why do they sell phones that have such an incredibly short lifetime? With new designs and handset functionality appearing all the time – and being heavily marketed by companies such as Nokia and Motorola – ask any kid in the playground how they feel about having an out-of-date phone, even to help the environment. On the high street, Marks & Sparks may be leading the pack in flogging T-shirts made from organic, fairtrade cotton, but isn't the whole idea of fashion the antithesis of a sustainable approach? As environmental author Paul Hawken says: 'Fashion is the deliberate inculcation of obsolescence.' Each new trend that sweeps the high street renders the old trend obsolete. It's difficult to imagine a more wasteful system.

This truth is illustrated well by what's actually going on in the real world, away from corporate press releases and catchy high-street initiatives. The sheer proliferation of electronic household gadgets means that electricity use and carbon emissions are still increasing every year. Energy use in the home has doubled in the past 30 years, and is projected to rise by another 12% by 2010. Whereas once the average house might have contained a fridge, a TV and a toaster, typical household gadgets now include power tools, phone chargers, dishwashers, microwaves, DVD players, computers, satellite receivers and Wi-Fi boxes. All these use energy, however efficient they might be individually – and most aren't very. The Energy Saving Trust has calculated that all the new entertainment and consumer electronics products in British households by 2020 will need another 14 average-sized power stations just to keep them running.

Some in the business community argue that the whole green consumerism thing is just a passing fad, a sort of climatic version of the dotcom bubble. 'If people do have an environmental conscience, you can buy it for a fiver,' boasts one anonymous airline executive. This cynicism seems to be backed up by a recent Mori poll, which showed that a majority of the British public still think – mistakenly – that scientists disagree on the reality of climate change, and that a significant number feel that the problem is overstated in order

to raise revenue for the government. According to Phil Downing, head of environmental research at Ipsos Mori, the majority of the population are 'fairweather environmentalists' who remain very reluctant to take lifestyle change seriously.

Moreover, some purportedly 'green' products may be even worse than those they are intended to replace. Tesco is positioning itself as the UK market leader in selling biofuels, and already offers a 5% bioethanol mix in 185 of its petrol stations. It is also adding biodiesel pumps to 181 of its filling stations in England. However, evidence suggests that biodiesel made from palm oil feedstock may be many times more carbon intensive than even fossil fuels, once the wholesale destruction of Indonesian rainforests for palm oil plantation is factored in to the carbon equation. Ethanol is mostly made from US corn, and supply constraints have pushed up world commodity prices, already making cornflour tortillas more expensive for the Mexican poor. In a globalised food economy, the harsh reality is that cars will be fed before people if the use of biofuels becomes significantly more widespread.

Another controversial attempt to try to resolve the contradiction between consumption and sustainability is carbon offsetting. Most of the big firms that trumpet their green credentials use offsetting to some extent: Sky's claim to be 'carbon neutral', for example, is justified by it having purchased carbon offsets up to the level of its calculated emissions. To help offset Barclays Bank's emissions, more than 30,000 trees have been planted in 'Barclays' Forests' around the country, also through the Carbon Neutral Company. But offsetting has come under fire as being little more than a conscience-salve, somewhat

akin to the purchasing of papal indulgences in the middle ages.

At the heart of green consumerism lies a single unanswered question: can ever-increasing resource consumption be truly reconciled with the ecological constraints of a fragile planet?

Many environmentalists are not impressed, and see green consumerism as at best a diversion, and at worst an intensification of ecologically damaging behaviour, 'a pox on the planet', in George Monbiot's words. 'Green consumerism is another form of atomisation – a substitute for collective action,' he writes. 'No political challenge can be met by shopping.' Monbiot claims that 'it is easy to picture a situation in which the whole world religiously buys green products and its carbon emissions continue to soar'. In this world, we would deceive ourselves by driving to the supermarket in a hybrid 4x4 to buy organic carrots, somehow believing that we were part of the solution rather than part of the problem. We would continue to forget that the first word in the green mantra of 'reduce, reuse and recycle' was always meant to be the most important.

Such ideas are not going to gain many converts among the corporate denizens of the high street – so one approach that has begun to catch on among the more radical elements of the green movement is to opt out of shopping altogether, and declare a 'Buy Nothing Day'. This year's is scheduled for 27 November; last year's saw samba bands march into shopping centres in Manchester, saboteurs in Oxford put stickers on clothes in Top Shop and Miss Selfridge declaring 'Put me down! I won't bring you happiness', and anti-consumerist carols sung in a shopping arcade in Bristol.

Declaring that 'less is more' may be appealing to some greens who are already suspicious of the consumer lifestyle, but whether a true mass movement can ever be built on a philosophy of voluntary simplicity is questionable at best. If Phil Downing from Mori is right and the majority of the population remain sceptical 'fairweather environmentalists', then clearly a lot more work remains to be done.

17 September 2007
© *Guardian Newspapers Limited 2007*

⇨ In our world today around 2.5 billion people do not have access to improved sanitation and some 1.2 billion people do not have access to an improved source of water. (page 1)

⇨ Population growth, along with high resource consumption by affluent populations, is contributing to increasing stress on the global environment. (page 2)

⇨ The increasing stress we put on resources and environmental systems such as water, land and air cannot go on for ever. Especially as the world's population continues to increase and we already see a world where over a billion people live on less than a dollar a day. (page 3)

⇨ 'Ecological debt day' is the date when, in effect, humanity uses up the resources the earth has available for that year, and begins eating into its stock of natural resources. World ecological debt day has crept ever earlier in the year since humanity first began living beyond its environmental means in the 1980s. (page 4)

⇨ Today we live in both a carbon constrained and water constrained world. Pressures on the environment are increasing as world population grows and parts of society become wealthier. The planet's renewable resources – like water, timber or fish – are rapidly being exhausted. (page 7)

⇨ Sustainability is a simple idea. It is based on the recognition that when resources are consumed faster than they are produced or renewed, the resource is depleted and eventually used up. (page 10)

⇨ The construction business in the UK is responsible for nearly a third of all industry-related pollution incidents. Construction and demolition waste alone represent 19% of total UK waste. (page 11)

⇨ The largest population increases and the most fragile environmental conditions are usually found in poor countries, which typically have limited financial means and least adequate political and managerial resources to address the challenges. (page 12)

⇨ Water crises, long seen as a problem of only the poorest, are increasingly affecting some of the world's wealthiest nations. (page 13)

⇨ Up against competition from such revolutionary developments as antibiotics, anaesthetic, vaccines and the understanding of DNA, the benefits of clean water and sewage disposal gained most votes from 11,000 doctors and members of the public questioned by the *British Medical Journal*. (page 15)

⇨ Recent waves of economic migrants into Europe are likely to be dwarfed by future flows of environmental refugees from drought-hit regions such as north Africa, according to a new study from the Optimum Population Trust. (page 16)

⇨ Between 2000 and 2030, the world's urban population is expected to increase by 72 per cent, while the built-up areas of cities of 100,000 people or more could increase by 175 per cent. (page 17)

⇨ From the dawn of agriculture, some 10,000 years ago, through the Industrial Revolution of the past three centuries, human beings have reshaped their landscapes on an ever-larger and lasting scale. (page 18)

⇨ Contaminated land is land that has been polluted with harmful substances to the point where it now poses a serious risk to human health and the environment. (page 22)

⇨ New figures show that Britain is officially the 'dustbin of Europe' as it dumps more household waste into landfill than any other country in the European Union. (page 23)

⇨ From the 1960s to 1990s the total area of England disturbed by the noise and visual intrusion of roads, urban areas and major infrastructure rose from 26% to 41%. (page 24)

⇨ It is not farming but poor farm management that affects the environment. Agriculture accounted for over 5% of pollution incidents in 2005. Poor land management results in soil erosion, and fertiliser and pesticide run-off that can cause pollution. Good management can reduce these impacts. (page 25)

⇨ Recent polls revealed that about 70% of the European public remained opposed to GM foods. (page 26)

⇨ Over-fishing is widely acknowledged to be one of the major threats to marine biodiversity. Currently 75% of global fish stocks are either fully exploited or over-fished. (page 28)

⇨ With only 8% of the world's ancient forests currently under strict protection, huge areas are still at risk from destructive logging. (page 31)

⇨ The European Union tops the list for major importer of many wild animal and plant products, including tropical timber, caviar, reptile skins and live reptiles. (page 34)

⇨ The major threat to clean air is now posed by traffic emissions. (page 35)

GLOSSARY

Biocapacity
A measure of an area's biological productivity.

Bycatch
Fish or other sea life caught unintentionally while fishing for other marine animals.

Capital flight
Money taken out of a country to be invested in a safer economy overseas.

Carbon offsetting
Paying someone to reduce carbon dioxide emissions to compensate for your emissions (e.g. by planting trees).

Consumption
Buying and using goods or services.

Degradation
Reduction of biological productivity or diversity.

Endemic
Native or restricted to a particular place.

Exploitation
The illegal or unfair use of resources for selfish reasons.

Expropriation
Taking property from its owner.

Fragmentation
When habitats are broken up into smaller areas by human development.

GDP (Gross Domestic Product)
The value of all goods and services produced in a country in a year.

Globalisation
Increasing connectivity and interdependence between individuals and countries globally.

Horticulture
Growing fruit, vegetables or decorative plants.

Incentivised
When a programme for recognising and rewarding good performance has been established.

Infrastructure
The facilities and services necessary for a site to be developed, such as water, sewers and roads.

Insolvency
When debts are greater than assets.

Interdependence
A relationship in which things depend on one another.

Mandate
Authority given to an elected representative to take action.

Marginalisation
A social process in which some people or groups are excluded.

Moratorium
A temporary ban on a specific activity.

NGO (non-governmental organisation)
An organisation that is usually non-profit and aims to influence government policy or the behaviour of a country's population.

Overshoot
When something goes beyond its limits or destination.

Precautionary principle
The view that when not all the information about a risk is known, avoidance or at least taking great care is necessary.

Privatisation
Changing from government-owned to privately-owned.

Proliferation
The rapid increase or multiplication of something.

Salinisation
An accumulation of salts, generally in soil or water.

Slums
Overcrowded, underdeveloped areas of housing where people live in poverty.

1,3-butadiene 36

agriculture
  effects on forests 30
  GM crops 26-7
  land use 25
  organic 25
  sustainable 27
agri-environment schemes 25
air pollution 35-6
  monitoring 37
anti-consumerism 39
aquaculture (fish farming) 29
Areas of Outstanding Natural Beauty (AONBs) 32
atmospheric changes, threats to biodiversity 19

benzene 36
biodiversity 18-21, 33
  protecting 20-21
  threats to 19, 21
  UK Biodiversity Action Plan 33
  value of 18-19
biofuels 39
biological resources 9
  see also biodiversity
bottom trawl fishing 28
building industry and sustainability 11
businesses
  and biodiversity protection 20
  and environmentalism 38-9
  sustainable 7
butadiene 36

carbon monoxide 36
carbon offsetting 39
certification schemes, timber 31
CITES (Convention on International Trade in Endangered Species of Wild Fauna and Flora) 34
climate change
  and biodiversity 19, 21
  Climate Change Programme 8
  and forests 30
conservation 32-3
construction, sustainable 11
consumerism, green 38-9
consumption, sustainable 7
contamination
  groundwater 36
  land 22
Convention on Biological Diversity 18, 20, 33
corporations and climate change 38-9
cultural identity and biological environment 19
deep water fisheries 28
deforestation 30-31
desertification, causing environmental migration 16
developing countries, money deposits in UK 6

development, effect on environment 24
diseases, water-associated 14, 15

ecological debt 4-6
ecological footprints 10, 17
ecological overshoot 10
ecosystem biodiversity 18, 19
energy consumption
  construction industry 11
  increasing 39
energy dependence, UK 5-6
environmental effects
  of agriculture 25
  of urban growth 17
environmental enhancement 9
environmental migration 16-17
environmental sustainability see sustainability
EU and wildlife trade 34

farmed fish 29
fertility rate and environmental stress 16-17
fine particles, air pollution 35
fish, buying 29
fisheries 28
food
  food security 12-13
  UK dependence on imports 5
foreign money deposits in UK 6
forests 30-31

genetic biodiversity 18
genetically modified crops 26-7
global interdependence 4-6
global warming, effects on biodiversity 19
GM crops 26-7
government action on forest destruction 30, 31
green consumerism 38-9
greenhouse gas emissions
  reduction targets 8-9
groundwater pollution 36

health workers from overseas, UK dependence on 6
heavy metals, air pollution 36
high seas bottom trawl fishing 28
household waste 23

imports, UK dependence on 4-6
individuals and biodiversity protection 21
interdependence, global 4-6
international trade, Britain's dependence on 4-6
International Year of Sanitation 15

Kyoto Protocol, UK target 8

landfill 23
lead pollution 36

Local Nature Reserves (LNRs) 32
logging, destructive 30

Millennium Development Goal 1-2

National Nature Reserves (NNRs) 32
National Parks 32
natural environment conservation 32-3
natural resources 9
nitrogen oxides 35

one planet economy 8
organic farming 25, 27
organic seafood 29
over fishing 28
overseas workers, UK dependence on 6
ozone and air pollution 35

pollution
  air 35-7
  water 36
population
  and environmental stress 16-17
  increase, effect on the environment 12-13
poverty and environmental stress 12
production, sustainable 7, 8
protected forest areas 31

resource efficiency 7
retailers and environmentalism 38

sanitation 14-15
Scotland, biodiversity threats 21
seafood, sustainable 29
Sky and environmentalism 38
soil loss, causing environmental migration 16
space
  as a natural resource 9
  sustainable 17
Special Areas of Conservation (SACs) 33
sulphur dioxide 35

sustainability 1-11
  agriculture 27
  construction industry 11
  consumption 7, 8
  definition 3
  production 7, 8
  seafood 29
  UK principles 3
  UK strategy 8-9
sustainable communities 9
Sustainable Development Strategy 8-9
sustainable use of space 17

timber production 30-31
toilets, lack of, developing countries 14-15
toxic organic micropollutants (TOMPS) 35-6
trade
  ecologically wasteful 5
  wildlife 34
traffic emissions 35

UK
  ecological debt 4-6
  natural environment conservation 32-3
  principles of sustainable development 3
  sustainable development strategy 8-9

urban growth 17, 24

waste
  construction industry 11
  household 23
water
  crises 13
  pollution 36
  security 12-13
  water-associated diseases 14, 15
wildlife
  conservation, UK 33
  global trade 34

Additional Resources

Other Issues *titles*

If you are interested in researching further some of the issues raised in *Sustainability and Environment*, you may like to read the following titles in the *Issues* series:
⇨ Vol. 151 *Climate Change* (ISBN 978 1 86168 424 0)
⇨ Vol. 150 *Migration and Population* (ISBN 978 1 86168 423 3)
⇨ Vol. 138 *A Genetically Modified Future?* (ISBN 978 1 86168 390 8)
⇨ Vol. 119 *Transport Trends* (ISBN 978 1 86168 352 6)
⇨ Vol. 111 *The Waste Problem* (ISBN 978 1 86168 344 1)
⇨ Vol. 97 *Energy Matters* (ISBN 978 1 86168 305 2)
⇨ Vol. 76 *The Water Crisis* (ISBN 978 1 86168 265 9)
For more information about these titles, visit our website at www.independence.co.uk/publicationslist

Useful organisations

You may find the websites of the following organisations useful for further research:
⇨ **Convention on Biological Diversity:** www.cbd.int
⇨ **Environment Agency:** www.environment-agency.gov.uk
⇨ **Global Footprint Network:** www.footprintnetwork.org
⇨ **Greenpeace:** www.greenpeace.org.uk
⇨ **nef (the new economics foundation):** www.neweconomics.org
⇨ **Soil Association:** www.soilassociation.org
⇨ **Sustainable Development:** www.sustainable-development.gov.uk
⇨ **United Nations Population Fund:** www.unfpa.org
⇨ **World Wildlife Fund:** www.wwf.org

ACKNOWLEDGEMENTS

The publisher is grateful for permission to reproduce the following material.

While every care has been taken to trace and acknowledge copyright, the publisher tenders its apology for any accidental infringement or where copyright has proved untraceable. The publisher would be pleased to come to a suitable arrangement in any such case with the rightful owner.

Chapter One: Defining Sustainability

Environmental sustainability, © UN Millennium Campaign, *Fast facts: environmental sustainability*, © United Nations Population Fund, *What is sustainable development?*, © Crown copyright is reproduced with the permission of Her Majesty's Stationery Office, *The UK's ecological debt*, © nef (the new economics foundation), *Sustainable consumption and production*, © Crown copyright is reproduced with the permission of Her Majesty's Stationery Office, *Securing the future*, © Crown copyright is reproduced with the permission of Her Majesty's Stationery Office, *What are natural resources?*, © Crown copyright is reproduced with the permission of Her Majesty's Stationery Office, *Ecological footprint*, © Global Footprint Network, *Sustainable construction*, © Environment Agency.

Chapter Two: Sustainability Challenges

Population, poverty and the environment, © United Nations Population Fund, *The water crisis*, © World Wildlife Fund, *2.6 billion wait in line for toilets*, © UN Millennium Campaign, *Plumbing beats penicillin*, © Associated Newspapers Ltd, *Environmental migration*, © Optimum Population Trust, *Urban growth and sustainable use of space*, © United Nations Population Fund, *Sustaining life on earth*, © Convention on Biological Diversity, *Your natural heritage: why it matters*, © Natural Scotland, *Contaminated land*, © Environment Agency, *Britain: the 'dustbin of Europe'*, © Crown copyright is reproduced with the permission of Her Majesty's Stationery Office, *Intrusion*, © Campaign to Protect Rural England, *Agricultural land use*, © Environment Agency, *What is organic?* © Soil Association, *Return of GM*, © Guardian Newspapers Ltd, *GM food: the solutions*, © Greenpeace, *Fisheries*, © Seas At Risk, *Better buys: what fish can I eat?*, © Greenpeace, *Forests*, © Greenpeace, *Conservation*, © Natural England, *EU: top global importer of wildlife*, © World Wildlife Fund, *Air pollution*, © UK Air Quality Archive, *Pollution putting groundwater at risk, warns agency*, © Guardian Newspapers Ltd, *Why monitor air pollution?*, © London Air Quality Network, *Can shopping save the planet?*, © Guardian Newspapers Ltd.

Photographs

Flickr: pages 4 (Dan H); 14 (le Korrigan); 21 (Mike Baird); 33 (ezioman).
Stock Xchng: pages 2 (Irum Shahid); 9 (Mary Bonney); 15 (Lance Hancock); 19 (Dave Sackville); 27a (Grzegorz Rejniak); 27b (Lars Sundström); 36 (Helmut Gevert); 39 (Sanja Gjenero).

Illustrations

Pages 1, 26: Angelo Madrid; pages 6, 37: Don Hatcher; pages 8, 11: Bev Aisbett; pages 10, 31: Simon Kneebone.

Additional research and editorial by Claire Owen on behalf of Independence.

And with thanks to the team: Mary Chapman, Sandra Dennis, Claire Owen and Jan Sunderland.

Cobi Smith and Lisa Firth
Cambridge
January, 2008